MEDICAL T...
WILL LEAVE YOU IN STITCHES

What does it mean to go on the Scarsdale Diet?
(see page 13)

Did you hear about the prostitute with a degree in psychiatry?
(see page 16)

What did the doctor say to the nympho-maniac?
(see page 19)

What do you call a cow that's had an abortion?
(see page 35)

How can you spot a disadvantaged doctor?
(see page 44)

How many doctors does it take to change a light bulb?
(see page 67)

Also by Blanche Knott
Published by St. Martin's Paperbacks

Blanche Knott's

Truly Tasteless Doctor Jokes

ST. MARTIN'S PAPERBACKS

BLANCHE KNOTT'S TRULY TASTELESS DOCTOR JOKES

ISBN: 0-312-92228-0

Printed in the United States of America

St. Martin's Paperbacks edition/June 1990

10 9 8 7 6 5 4 3 2 1

To Dr. Coffey

Truly
Tasteless
Doctor
Jokes

Jerry had gone in for a routine checkup, and when he came back in for the results his doctor sounded very solemn indeed. "I think you'd better sit down, Jerry. I've got some good news and some bad news."

"Okay, Doc," said the patient, steeling himself. "Give me the bad news."

"You've got cancer. It's metastasized widely, it's spreading unbelievably fast, it's totally inoperable, and you've got a month or less left to live."

"Jesus Christ," gasped Jerry, wiping the cold sweat off his forehead. "What the hell's the good news?"

"You know that really cute new receptionist out in the front office?" asked the doctor.

"Sure do," answered Jerry.

"The one with the big tits and that adorable ass?"

"Yup."

"And the long, gorgeous blonde hair?"

"Yeah, yeah," said Jerry impatiently.

"Well," said the doctor, leaning forward with a grin, "I'm screwing her!"

•

The patient cleared his throat a little embarrassedly before explaining his rather unusual problem. "YOU SEE, DOC," he boomed in a voice so deep and raspy it was almost impossible to understand, "I CAN'T GO ON WITH THIS VOICE ANYMORE—IT'S DRIVING ME CRAZY! CAN YOU FIX IT SO I SOUND LIKE A NORMAL PERSON?"

"I'll certainly try," said Doctor Addison comfortingly. After examining the patient, he reported that some sort of weight was pulling on the vocal cords and distorting the voice. "Any idea what it could be?" he queried.

The patient cleared his throat again. "ACTUALLY, DOC, I HAPPEN TO BE . . . UH . . . ESPECIALLY WELL-ENDOWED, AND MAYBE THAT'S WHAT'S DOING IT! LISTEN, IF YOU HAVE TO REMOVE SOME OF IT, THAT'S FINE BY ME! I'LL DO *ANYTHING* TO GET A VOICE LIKE A REGULAR GUY!" So the doctor went ahead and performed the operation.

Two weeks later the patient telephoned the doctor's office. "Hey, Doc," he babbled happily, "I can't thank you enough. Finally I sound like anyone else, I can lead a normal life—it's just great! Say, by the way, Doctor Addison, what'd you do with the piece of my penis you removed?"

"I THREW IT AWAY!"

•

Doctor (taking up his stethoscope): "Big breaths."
Patient: "Yeth, and I'm not even thixteen."

•

Hear about the famous Polish doctor?

He performed the first successful hemorrhoid transplant.

•

What did the doctor tell Rock Hudson when he contracted AIDS?

"Don't worry, you'll be back on your knees in no time."

•

Two very nervous young men got to talking in the doctor's waiting room and discovered they had somewhat similar symptoms: one had a red ring around the base of his penis, and the other one a green ring. The fellow with the red ring was examined first, and came out all smiles in a few minutes. "Don't worry, man, it's nothing!" he announced cheerfully.

Vastly relieved, the second patient went in to the examining room, only to have the doctor tell him a few minutes later, "I'm very sorry, but you have an advanced case of V.D. Your penis will have to be amputated."

Turning white as a sheet, the young man gasped, "But the first guy . . . he said it was no big deal!"

"Well, you know," the doctor pointed out, "there's a big difference between lipstick and gangrene."

•

At the doctor for an examination, this guy pulls down his pants to expose a penis the size of an olive. When the doctor and nurse crack up, the guy snaps, "Whatsa matter, never seen a hard-on before?"

•

Explaining to his doctor that his sex life wasn't all it could be, Milt asked for a pill that would enable him to get it up for his wife. The doctor knew just what to prescribe, so Milt went by the pharmacy, took a pill and drove home. But when he got to the apartment his wife wasn't there, and after waiting for an hour or so in growing discomfort, Milt finally had to jerk off.

When the doctor called to check in the next day, Milt explained what had happened. "Well, gee, Milt, you didn't have to do it yourself," pointed out the doctor. "There are other women in the building."

"Doctor," said Milt, "for other women I don't need a pill."

•

Hear about the woman who was so ugly that when she was born, the doctor slapped her mother?

•

A gay goes to the proctologist for a routine examination. When the doctor gets him into position, he's quite surprised to find a piece of string dangling from the man's ass. He pulls gently and out pops a lovely bouquet of flowers.

"Do you know I just pulled a dozen roses out of your rectum?" asks the astonished doctor.

"Is that so?" muses the patient. "Who are they from?"

•

An old man went to bed one night and put his glass eye in a cup. In the middle of the night, he drank the water and inadvertently swallowed the glass eye. Waking up and realizing what he had done, he tottered over to the doctor's office and asked him to retrieve it. Probing every orifice of the old codger's body, the doctor finally asked him to bend over so he could find out if the elusive glass eye was located in the man's rectum—as indeed it was.

"Do you see it yet, Doc?" asked the old coot.

"No," replied the doctor, probing further.

"That's funny, because I can see you real well!" he hooted.

•

"Doctor," an old man complained, "I can't pee."

"Hmmm," contemplated the doctor, "How old are you?"

"Eighty-seven," the aged fellow replied.

"Well, haven't you peed enough?"

A horny young couple was touring New England, and when they visited a historic cemetery they couldn't resist screwing vigorously on the long flat tombstones. The next day, though, the girl visited a local doctor complaining of a backache.

After asking her to disrobe and examining her thoroughly, the doctor couldn't find anything wrong with her. "But by the way," he asked, "how old are you?"

"Twenty-four," she replied. "Why?"

The doctor said, "Well, it says on your ass you died in 1787."

•

The myopic little girl went to the doctor for her first eye examination. Too young to really know how to spell when the doctor asked her to read from his chart, she very carefully spelled out "a–s–s."

Startled, the doctor looked up and remarked, "Well, that's the first time I knew that I sat on my 4–b–6!"

•

"You just have minor cuts on your buttocks," the doctor reported. "What happened?"

"Well, you see," the patient explained, "I was screwing my girlfriend when all of a sudden, the chandelier fell."

"Wow!" exclaimed the doctor. "You're a very lucky man."

"You're telling me!" the patient said with a sigh of relief. "A minute sooner and I would have had a fractured skull!"

•

Stanley and Ania got married and wanted desperately to make love and have a baby, but, being Polish, they had never been taught how to "do it." So Stanley finally sought the services of Poland's greatest sex therapist, Dr. Shenkowski.

Sitting the young man down in his office, Dr. Shenkoswki said grandly, "Stanley, making love is one of the finest things than can take place between a man and a woman in marriage . . ."

"I know, Doctor, but could you please tell me exactly how to go about it?" interrupted Stanley, embarrassed but determined.

Shenkowski realized he'd better make it simple. "Okay, Stanley, you, as a man, take the longest thing on your body and stick it into the hairiest part of hers," he instructed. "You'll get the knack of it soon enough." He patted his patient on the back and showed him out.

Two months later a pissed-off Stanley walked back into his office. "Dr. Shenkowski," he yelled,

"I've been following your instructions every night and Ania's still not pregnant. And frankly, I don't think this sex business is all it's cracked up to be! Some doctor you are."

"Now, Stanley," said Dr. Shenkowski soothingly, "calm down and tell me exactly what went on between you two. I'm sure I can sort things out."

"Don't try and blame it on me," blustered Stanley. "I followed your directions to the letter. Every single night I stuck my nose as far as it would go into her armpit!"

•

After consulting the doctor and the rabbi, the concerned husband came home and sheepishly told his wife that he'd contracted a bad case of gonorrhea. Thoroughly perplexed, the somewhat naive Mrs. Goldfarb went straight to the dictionary and looked it up.

"Shemp," she announced triumphantly, "you have nothing to worry about. It says right here that 'gonorrhea' is an inflammation of the Gentiles!"

•

What's a Jewish mother's dilemma?
Having a gay son who's dating a doctor.

Sergeant Mack had a fine time during his stay in Hong Kong, but paid for it when he came down with a strange Oriental venereal disease. So he made the rounds of every American doctor in the community. To his horror he discovered that not only were they unable to cure him, each informed him that the only course of treatment was amputation of the penis.

Desperate, Sergeant Mack made an appointment with a leading Chinese doctor, figuring that he might know more about an Eastern malady. "Doctor Cheung, do you think I need to have my dick cut off?" he asked anxiously.

"No, no, no," said the Chinese doctor testily.

A huge smile broke out over the serviceman's face. "Boy, that's *great*, Doc. Every one of those American medics said they'd have to cut it off."

"Those Western doctors—all they ever want to do is cut, cut cut," explained Dr. Cheung, exasperated. "You just wait two weeks. Penis fall off all by itself."

•

When Bridget complained to the doctor of severe intestinal pains, he told her he needed a sample. "And what does he mean by that?" she asked her husband over dinner that night.

"I wouldn't be knowing," admitted her husband. "You'd best ask Katherine."

Now Katherine had lived in Dublin and was forever putting on airs about her worldliness, and Bridget hated asking her anything, but she didn't know who else to turn to. So off she went to Katherine's house, only to return half an hour later all battered and scratched.

"An' what happened to ye?" asked her startled husband.

"She tol' me to go pee in a bottle," reported Bridget, blushing scarlet, "so I told her to go shit in her hat."

•

Feeling romantic one day, Stan brought his lover home a beautiful bunch of roses, but they brought on a tremendous attack of sneezing and wheezing. "I didn't used to be allergic to roses," gasped Teddy, blowing his nose.

Stan was still feeling romantic the next day and came home with a beautiful bouquet of lilies, but they had the same effect. And when an armful of chrysanthemums sent Teddy straight to bed, Stan lost his temper. "This is ridiculous," he snapped. "You should see a doctor."

So Teddy made an appointment with a well-known allergist, bringing the suspect bouquets with him. After a series of tests, the doctor called Teddy into his office.

"What should I do, Doctor?" asked Teddy. "We're desperate."

"Get your boyfriend to change florists," advised the allergist. "This one uses pussy willows in his arrangements."

•

An elderly man with a hearing problem suddenly went completely deaf in one ear. Concerned, he went to the ENT specialist, who looked in his ear, picked up a pair of forceps, and extracted a suppository.

"Here's the trouble," the doctor announced, showing it to him.

The old man sighed in relief. "Now I know what I did with my hearing aid!"

•

Beset with grief, a poor homosexual had just found out that he had AIDS. "What am I going to do?" pleaded the man after his doctor had reviewed the prognosis.

"I think you should go to Mexico and live it up. Drink the water and eat all the Mexican cuisine you can get your hands on, including raw fruits and vegetables," advised the doctor.

"Oh, God, Doc, will that cure me?" asked the gay.

"No," answered the doctor candidly, "but it'll teach you what your asshole is for."

A homosexual gets some suppositories from his doctor, but he's not sure how to go about inserting them.

"Before you get dressed in the morning," the doctor instructs, "stand on a mirror and bend over. You should have no problem."

So the next morning when he gets out of bed, the fag takes his mirror down off the wall and stands on it. Suddenly, he gets a terrific boner. Chuckling, the fag looks down and murmurs fondly, "It's just me, silly."

What does it mean to go on the Scarsdale Diet?

You shoot your doctor and then spend the rest of your life eating bread and water.

A man with a frog perched on top of his head goes to see a doctor.

"What seems to be the problem?" the physician asks.

"My ass," says the frog.

"And . . . uh . . . what's wrong with your ass?"

13

the doctor inquires further, amazed to be conversing with a frog.

"Would you believe," complains the frog, "this started as a wart?"

•

With one look at his voluptuous new patient, all the gynecologist's professional ethics went right out the window. Instructing her to undress completely, he began to stroke the soft skin of her inner thigh. "Do you know what I'm doing?" he asked softly.

"Checking for any dermatological abnormalities, right?"

"Right," crooned the doctor, beginning to fondle her breasts and gently pinch her nipples. "And now?"

"Looking for any lumps that might be cancerous."

"Right you are," reassured the doctor, placing her feet in the stirrups, pulling out his cock, and entering her. "And do you know what I'm doing now?"

"Yup," she replied, "catching herpes."

•

An assembly-line worker became increasingly obsessed with his desire to stick his penis into the pickle slicer. Finally, worried that he'd be unable to contain the desire, he sought the advice of a psychiatrist.

"You know, I had a case not unlike this one a few months ago," said Dr. Bernstein, thoughtfully rubbing his beard, "a man who kept wanting to put his hand on a hot stove."

"So what happened?" asked the factory worker.

"He went ahead and did it," confessed the doctor, "and he burned himself but he never had the desire again. So my advice is to go ahead and do it in order to free yourself of the obsession."

"Okay, Dr. Bernstein."

At his next appointment the doctor asked what had happened.

"I took your advice," said the man, "and stuck my penis into the pickle slicer."

"So then what happened?" asked the psychiatrist, leaning forward eagerly.

"We both got fired."

•

How much did the psychiatrist charge the elephant?

$385.

$35 for the visit and $350 for the sofa.

•

Did you hear about the prostitute with a degree in psychiatry?

She'll blow your mind.

●

A man was experiencing chronic infections so he took his urologist's advice and entered the hospital for a routine circumcision. When he came to, he was perturbed to see a large group of doctors standing around his hospital bed. "What's the problem, Doc?" he asked nervously.

"Uh, well . . . there's been a bit of a mix-up," admitted his surgeon. "I'm afraid that instead of a circumcision, we performed a sex-change operation on you. You now have a very nice vagina instead of a penis."

"What!" gasped the patient. "You mean I'll never experience another erection?"

"Oh, I'm *sure* you will," reassured the doctor promptly. "It'll just be somebody else's."

●

When Mike came into the office for the results of some medical tests, the doctor told him he had some good news and some bad news. Mike asked for the good news first.

"Your penis is going to grow two inches in length

and an inch in circumference," the doctor informed him.

"That's terrific," Mike exclaimed, breaking into a big smile. "So what could be bad?"

"Malignant."

•

"The doctor said I have the legs of a seventeen-year-old!" announced the old woman triumphantly to her husband.

"Big deal," her husband chuckled sarcastically. "What did he say about your sixty-five-year-old ass?"

"Oh," she retorted, "you didn't come up in the conversation."

•

"Doctor, I'm losing my sex urge," complained Ruth at her annual checkup.

"Mrs. Beeston, that's understandable at eighty-four," said the doctor, "but tell me: when did you first start noticing this?"

"Last night," she answered, "and then again this morning."

"Aha!" said the doctor. "Your problem isn't a diminished sex drive—it's that you're not getting enough. You should be having sex at least fifteen times a month."

Thanking him and heading home, the old woman couldn't wait to report to her husband. "Guess what, Pop? Dr. North says I need it fifteen times a month!"

Pop put in his teeth and responded, "That's just great, honey. Put me down for five."

•

"I'm afraid I have to operate immediately," pronounced the dentist gravely.

"But, Doctor, this was just a routine check-up," protested the patient. "I feel terrific!"

"That just goes to show why check-ups are such a good idea," explained the dentist. "This condition might have killed you. Even as is, it's going to be a long and difficult oral surgery procedure, and it's going to cost you ten thousand dollars."

The patient paled. "I don't have that kind of money," he protested weakly.

"That's okay," said the dentist soothingly. "It doesn't have to be paid in full. We can arrange a monthly installment plan."

"Oh, I see . . . Sort of like buying a car?"

"Yeah," said the dentist, "I am."

•

The obstetrician was surprised when the husband of one of his patients requested an appoint-

18

ment. When the time came he ushered him into his office and asked, "What can I do for you?"

"Doc," confessed the husband, "I'm worried because our new baby has red hair."

"Why is that a cause for concern?" asked the doctor.

"Well, I have black hair, my wife has black hair, and all four grandparents have black hair."

The doctor thought for a minute or two. "How often do you and your wife have sex?" he asked.

"About twice a year."

"That explains it," proclaimed the obstetrician. "The red hair is rust."

.

When the doctor answered his phone, a frantic father was on the other end. "Come quick, Doc, my little boy just swallowed a rubber!"

The doctor hung up, grabbed his bag, and was running for the door when the phone rang again.

"Never mind, Doc," said the boy's father. "I found another one."

.

What did the doctor say to the nymphomaniac?

"Take two aspirin and ball me in the morning."

When is a doctor the most annoyed?
When he's out of patients.

How did the shrink greet his fellow psychiatrist when they met on the street?
"You're fine—how am I?"

The gynecologist stuck up his head after completing his examination. "I'm sorry, Miss," he said, "but removing that vibrator is going to involve a very lengthy and delicate operation."

"I'm not sure I can afford it," sighed the young woman on the examining table. "Why don't you just replace the batteries?"

What does a gay nurse give his patients?
First-AIDS.

What should you look for when buying a one-ton canary?

A psychiatrist.

•

Two Polish guys went away on their annual hunting expedition, and by accident one shot another in the stomach. Panicked, the man who fired the shot dragged his pal out of the woods, into the car, and off to the closest hospital.

When the examining surgeon came out of the operating room, the fellow rushed over. "Is my friend going to make it?"

"It's a tough case," the doctor admitted frankly. "He'd have a better chance if you hadn't gutted him first."

•

How come Italians don't become pharmacists?

They can't fit the little bottles in the typewriter.

•

Did you hear about the unattractive medical student who went in for a penis transplant?

His hand rejected it.

•

A racist Southern planter went into the hospital and was informed by the doctor that his condition was grave. "In fact, old friend," the doctor said gravely, "a bypass operation won't do the job—you need a complete heart transplant."

"Whatever you say, Doc," drawled the patient philosophically. "But whatever you do, just don't give me a nigger's heart." And he was wheeled off to the operating room.

When he came to, the doctor was leaning over him anxiously. "I've got some good news and some bad news, Cal. The bad news is that a black man's heart was the only one available."

Cal paled.

"But the good news is that your dick's grown three inches!"

•

How come there are so few Hispanic doctors?

Because you can't write prescriptions with spray paint.

A homosexual was riding along in the subway when he caught sight of a man who was so handsome that he fell in love on the spot. Following him out of the station, he trailed him into a building and up to his office. What luck—the object of his desire was a proctologist! He went right in and made an appointment.

But as the examination progressed, the gay's moans of evident pleasure infuriated the doctor. "My job is to heal the sick, not provide sexual favors," he shouted, and tossed the would-be patient out of his office.

Not easily dissuaded, the lovelorn fag soon telephoned to set up another appointment, this time claiming an acute medical problem and insisting he needed the doctor's services. The proctologist reluctantly consented. Beginning the examination, he was astonished to find a long, thorny green stem protruding from the patient's asshole . . . then another . . . then another . . .

"My God," cried the doctor, "you've got a dozen red roses up your ass! Now I warned you I was a reputable medical practitioner—just what sort of tricks are you up to?"

"Read the card," gasped the fag, "read the card!"

filthy !

Two gay plastic surgeons were having dinner when one leaned over and confided, "You know, I just got myself circumcised two weeks ago."

"Marvelous! You must let me see it."

His friend obliged, discreetly pulling down his shorts and lifting the tablecloth.

"Ooooh," gasped his dinner companion admiringly. "You look ten years younger!"

•

The nervous father-to-be was pacing outside the delivery room door when finally the doctor emerged. "Thank God!" he cried. "Is it a boy or a girl?"

"Sit down, Bob," advised the doctor. "I'm afraid I have some bad news: I'm sorry to have to tell you that your child was not born anatomically complete."

Bob's face fell, but he soon cheered up. "Well, they can do amazing surgery on hermaphrodites these days, right? I'm sure it'll be able to lead a normal life."

"That's not all of it, Bob. Your child was born with no arms or legs."

Bob gasped, but then he pointed out the remarkable progress being made with artificial limbs.

The doctor patted him on the arm and nodded reassuringly. "But I'm afraid it's still not going to be easy, Bob. Your child was born with no torso. In fact, your child is only a giant ear."

Bob moaned and put his hands over his face—but in a few minutes he'd regained his composure.

"My wife is a wonderful woman, Doctor, and she and I will make the best of it somehow," he declared bravely.

"There's just one more thing, Bob. It's deaf."

•

Then there's the sad story of the poor young fellow who was in a terrible motorcycle accident. When he came out from under the anaesthetic, the doctor was leaning over him sympathetically.

"Son," he said kindly, "I've got to break some terrible news to you, but I have some good news too. The bad news is that you were in a terrible accident, and we had to amputate both legs below the knee."

"Jesus," gasped the lad. "What's the good news— I could use it."

"See that fellow in the bed across the aisle? He'd like to buy your boots."

•

Harry came into work on Monday feeling absolutely fine, and so was astonished when his secretary took one look at him and urged him to lie down on the couch. He was even more surprised when his boss came in and ordered him to take the day off, if not the week. Even his poker buddies wouldn't have anything to do with him that night,

insisting he go straight to bed. Finally, tired of re-
sisting everyone's advice, he went to see his internist, who took one look at him and rushed over
with a stretcher.

"But Doctor," Harry protested, "I *feel* fine."

This was a puzzler, conceded the doctor, who
proceeded to refer to the enormous reference
tomes behind his desk, muttering to himself,
"Looks good, feels good . . . no, you look like
hell. Looks good, feels terrible . . . nope, you say
you're feeling great, right?" Thumbing furiously
through volume after volume, the doctor went on,
"Looks terrible, feels terrible . . . no, that's not it
either." Finally, "Looks terrible, feels great."

"Aha!" he cried, looking up with a triumphant
smile. "You're a vagina!"

•

Why do dentists count so many Polish women
among their patients?

Because when the women use vibrators, they
chip their teeth.

•

You know how these days everyone wants a second opinion? Well, this lady had been going to a
psychiatrist for years, and one day she decided
she'd had enough of it. "Doctor," she announced,

walking into his office one morning, "I've been seeing you every Thursday for five years now. I don't feel any better; I don't feel any worse. What's the story? Give it to me straight—what's wrong with me?"

"Okay, I'll tell you: you're crazy," replied the shrink matter-of-factly.

"Now wait just a minute," protested the woman. "I want a second opinion."

"Fine," said the doctor. "You're ugly too."

•

Did you hear about the blind gynecologist?
   He could read lips.

•

The harried resident was walking down the hospital corridor when the head nurse stopped him. "Dr. Mills," she whispered, "you've got a thermometer stuck behind your ear."

"Shit!" he yelled. "Some asshole has my pen!"

•

27

Routine circumcisions were part of a certain country doctor's job, and he found himself oddly reluctant to throw the foreskins away. So he saved them all up in a jar of formaldehyde for many years, until it came time for the doctor to retire. And as he was cleaning out his office, he came across the jar full of foreskins, which by this time was nearly full. It seemed a pity to discard them after all this time, so he took them down to the tailor's shop and asked whether he could make something out of them.

"No problem," the tailor assured him. "Come back a week from Tuesday." And on that day the tailor proudly presented the elderly man with a fine wallet.

"Now wait just a minute," protested the disappointed doctor. "There were literally hundreds of foreskins in that jar, and all I've got to show for them is a measly *wallet?*"

"Calm down," soothed the tailor. "Rub it for a minute or so and it turns into a briefcase."

•

This young man decided that he simply wasn't adequately endowed, so he went to a doctor and announced his desire to have his penis surgically enlarged. The surgeon informed him that the only means of significantly enlarging matters would be to implant a section of a baby elephant's trunk, and that this was still a somewhat experimental procedure.

Rather a radical solution, agreed the young man,

but he was adamant. The operation was performed without complications, and within a few weeks the patient decided it was time to try out his new equipment. He asked a lovely young woman of his acquaintance out to dinner at an elegant restaurant. They were quietly chatting over a chilled Chablis when his new organ, which had been comfortably resting in his left pant leg, whipped out over the table, grabbed a hard roll, and just as speedily disappeared back under the tablecloth.

"Wow!" gasped the young woman, truly impressed. "Could you do that again?"

"Sure," he replied, trying to act nonchalant, "but I don't think my asshole can stand another hard roll."

•

There was once a young man who was so fixated on the female breast that he decided to seek professional help. The first test the psychiatrist performed was one of simple word association. "Just say the first word that comes to mind," instructed the doctor. "Orange."

"Breast," said the young man.

"Plum."

"Breast."

"Grapefruit."

"Breast."

"Windshield wipers."

"Breast."

"Now hang on a sec," interjected the psychiatrist. "Oranges I can see reminding you of breasts.

29

Grapefruit too; plums if you're stretching it. But windshield wipers?"

"Sure," explained the patient. "First this one, then that one. . . ."

•

What's the worst thing for a JAP about having a colostomy?

It's so *difficult* to find shoes to match the bag.

•

Why do Polish doctors make lousy lovers?

They always wait for the swelling to go down.

•

An international convention of sexologists was convened to determine once and for all why the human penis is shaped the way it is. Each national delegation had conducted extensive research and was to announce its results.

Said the French doctor, "We have spent fifty million francs and can now firmly say zat ze penis is ze shape eet is in order to give pleasure to ze woman."

"I say," spoke up the British spokesperson, "we've spent thirty thousand pounds and are dead certain that the male organ is that shape in order to give maximum pleasure to the fellow himself."

"Well, we've spent a million bucks," drawled the American doctor, "and there's no further doubt about the fact that it's that shape so your hand doesn't slip off the end."

•

A woman sought the advice of a sex therapist, confiding that she was finding it increasingly difficult to find a man who could satisfy her and that getting in and out of all these short-term relationships was growing wearisome. "Isn't there some way to judge the size of a man's equipment from the outside?" she asked.

"The only foolproof way is by the size of his feet," the doctor informed her.

So the woman proceeded to go downtown and cruise the streets until she came across a young man with the biggest feet she'd ever seen. She wined him and dined him and took him back to her apartment, all aflutter at the prospect of a night of sexual ecstasy.

When the fellow woke up the next morning, the woman had already gone out. On the bedside table was $40 and a note that read, "With my compliments, take this money and go out and buy a pair of shoes that fit you."

This 600-pound guy decides he can't go on living this way, so he seeks the help of a clinic and proceeds to go on a drastic diet. It works: four months later the guy's down to 180 pounds and feeling great. There's just one problem—he's covered with great folds of flesh which had once been filled by fat.

When he calls the clinic, the doctor urges him there's no cause for concern. "There's a special surgical procedure to correct this condition. Just come on over."

"But, Doctor," explains the erstwhile fatty, "you don't understand how weird I look. I'm too embarrassed to be seen in public."

"Don't give it another thought," the doctor says firmly. "Just pull up all the skin as high as you can, pile it on top of your head, put on a hat, and get over to the clinic." So the patient follows his instructions, provoking no comments until he's standing in front of the admitting nurse's desk, dying of self-consciousness.

"The doctor will be right with you, Mr. Greene," she tells him. "Please have a seat. Say, what's that hole in the middle of your forehead?"

"My belly button," blurted the miserable fellow. "How d'you like my tie?"

This well-to-do suburban matron's gynecologist retired, so when it came time for her annual checkup, she sought the services of a new practitioner.

Following the examination, he called her into his office. "You'll be glad to know that everything is in perfect condition," the new doctor reported cheerily. "In fact, you've got the cleanest vagina I've ever seen."

"It should be," she snapped. "I've got a colored man coming in twice a week."

•

Fred's wife refused to wear underwear and it drove him crazy. He didn't think it was proper or sanitary or healthy, but nothing he said persuaded her to mend her ways.

One winter she caught a bad cold, and Fred had a brainstorm. Calling up the family doctor, he explained his hangup and his wife's condition. "I'd really appreciate your coming over to look in on June, Dr. Brenner, and if you could somehow persuade her that the illness was linked to that unfortunate habit of hers, why, I'd be happy to double your fee."

The doctor came over and found the patient wrapped in a blanket on the living room sofa, sneezing and blowing her nose. He checked her ears, listened to her chest, looked down her throat, and announced solemnly, "Mrs. Gates, I'll give you an antibiotic for this infection—but if you don't start wearing underwear, this congestion could hang on till spring."

Mrs. Gates looked up at him skeptically. "You mean to tell me, Dr. Brenner, that you can tell from looking down my throat that I'm not wearing panties?"

Brenner cleared his throat modestly and assured her that that was indeed the case.

"Well, then," she retorted, "would you mind looking up my ass to see if my hat's on straight?"

•

Why do fertility experts think test-tube babies are so lucky?

Because they've got wombs with a view.

•

Two gay men decided that their lives would be complete only if they had a baby. So they found an obliging lesbian, donated the sperm with which she was impregnated, and were simply thrilled when she gave birth to an eight-pound boy. They rushed over to the hospital for the first viewing of their son, and stood with noses pressed against the nursery window, surveying row upon row of squalling newborns.

Only one baby was quiet, cooing softly to himself, and sure enough, that was the one the nurse brought over to the window for them to admire. One of the new fathers couldn't resist boasting a bit. "He sure is well behaved compared to these other howling brats, eh?"

"Oh, he's quiet now," replied the nurse, "but he squalls like all the rest when I take the pacifier out of his ass."

•

Did you hear Grace Kelly and Patricia Neal were to have made a movie together?

It was going to be called *Different Strokes*.

•

What do you call a cow that's had an abortion?
Decaffeinated.

•

This guy walks into a psychiatrist's office with a duck on his head.

"May I help you?" inquires the doctor politely, trying not to stare.

"Yeah," snaps the duck. "Get this guy off my ass."

35

The young couple had been married less than a year when they came in to see the doctor. The husband was obviously embarrassed, but nevertheless made it clear that the appointment had been his idea. "You see, Doctor," he confided, "my wife, she eats like a horse."

"There's absolutely no cause for concern," reassured the doctor. "Many healthy young women have hearty appetites."

"Oh, I know that, Doctor. But my wife spends her days on all fours in the barn, and all she'll eat is barley, oats, and alfalfa."

"Hmmmmm," mused the doctor, and leaned back in her chair. After reflecting for a few moments, she took out a piece of paper and began scribbling away.

The young husband perked up noticeably. "Can you cure her, Doctor?" he asked eagerly. "Are you writing out some sort of prescription?"

"Certainly not," replied the doctor. "It's a permit so she can shit in the streets."

•

~Greg's divorce left him lonely and horny, but after so many years away from the dating scene he was a little awkward about how to proceed. Still, with his doctor's encouragement, he did start to go out on a regular basis.

One Saturday night the doctor's phone rang. "I'm sorry to bother you at home," blurted Greg, obviously rather agitated, "but I just *had* to have your advice right away. See, I've met this terrific woman, we get along great, I really think she could be the one for me, everything's going great—"

"So?" interrupted the doctor, trying to conceal his irritation at having been summoned away from the dinner table.

"There's one little problem," Greg explained. "I really want to take her home with me, but I can't remember from our first date whether she said she had V.D. or T.B. What should I do?"

The doctor thought for a moment, then advised, "If she coughs, fuck her."

•

What did the womanizing dentist use for dental floss?

Pubic hair.

•

After a long day at a medical convention in Geneva, several doctors were comparing notes over dinner in a swank restaurant. An Israeli surgeon boasted, "Medicine in my country is so advanced that we can take a kidney out of one person, put it

37

into another, and have her up and looking for work six weeks later."

"That's nothing," maintained a practitioner from Munich. "In Germany we can transplant a lung and have both donor and recipient out looking for work in a month."

The Soviet doctor announced that at the Moscow Institute a human heart had been cut in half and successfully transplanted. "And both patients were up and looking for work in two weeks," she bragged.

"Shucks, that's nothing," said the American doctor. "We can take an asshole out of Yale and have millions of people out looking for work the next day!"

•

At her annual checkup, the attractive young woman was informed that it was necessary to have her temperature taken rectally. She agreed, but a few moments later cried indignantly, "Doctor, that's not my rectum!"

"And it's not my thermometer, either," admitted the doctor with a grin.

Just then the woman's husband, who had come to pick her up, walked into the examining room. "What the hell's going on here?" he demanded.

"Just taking your wife's temperature," the doctor explained coolly.

"Okay, Doc," grumbled the fellow, "but that thing better have numbers on it!"

Over lunch at the golf club, three retired gastro-enterologists were debating whose ailments and afflictions were the worst. "Have I got a problem?" the seventy-year-old complained. "Every morning I get up at 7:30 and have to take a piss, but then I have to stand at the toilet for an hour because my pee barely trickles out."

"Heck, that's nothing," maintained the eighty-year-old. "Every morning at 8:30 I have to take a dump, but I'm so constipated I have to sit on the can for an hour and a half. It's terrible."

The ninety-year-old moaned, "And you guys think you have it rough? Every morning at 7:30 I piss like a racehorse, and at 8:30 I shit like a pig."

"So what's the problem?" asked his buddies indignantly.

"I don't wake up till ten."

•

The homosexual made an appointment with his urologist and said, "Dr. Briggs, I think I've got V.D."

"From whom?" asked the physician.

"How should I know? You think I've got eyes in the back of my head?"

•

An insurance salesman dies and goes to heaven, only to find a long, long line ahead of him at the Pearly Gates. He waits and waits for hours, talking to the others in line: cops, clerks, people from every walk of life. As they're chatting and comparing notes on their lives and deaths, they catch sight of a man in white, carrying a black bag, who pushes his way to the head of the line. And after exchanging a few words with St. Peter, the fellow is immediately ushered into Heaven.

The salesman is irate. Never having let himself be pushed around in life, he isn't about to start letting it happen now, so he marches over to St. Peter and gives him a piece of his mind. "How come all the rest of us ordinary folks wait patiently in line and that asshole gets to barge ahead like he's something special?" he roars.

"Now, now, calm down," soothes St. Peter. "That was just God playing doctor."

•

The arrogant young cardiologist was no favorite among the nurses, whom he treated strictly as second-class citizens. So they were surprised and pleased when he fell madly in love with a sweet young thing, in pursuit of whom all his macho traits fell by the wayside.

The couple got married, and for months the doctor asked, pleaded, and begged for his bride to go down on him. But to no avail, for the young woman was simply too innocent and inexperienced even to *consider* such an activity. But a year of gentle persistence finally paid off, and finally his sweetheart nervously but lovingly performed the act. When it was over she looked up tenderly and asked, "How was I, darling?"

"How should I know?" he shot back. "I'm no cocksucker."

•

A urologist claimed that he could detect any disease simply by testing the patient's urine, so his pal Joey, who suffered from tennis elbow, decided to pull a prank on him. He made an appointment, received his specimen bottle, and was told to bring it back full the next morning.

That night he peed in the bottle, and so did his wife, his daughter, and the family dog. The next morning Joey jerked off in the bottle to top it off, then innocently handed it over to the receptionist.

Four days went by before the urologist reported back to Joey. "I had a hell of a time with this one," he admitted, "but I think I've got it. Your wife has the clap, your daughter is pregnant, your dog has worms, and if you'd quit jerking off, you wouldn't have tennis elbow."

•

During World War II, a badly wounded German officer was transferred to a Polish medical unit stationed in the United States. Fortunately for the wounded man, an American surgeon was placed in charge of his case, but his injuries were so severe that gangrene had already set in. Told that his left arm needed to be amputated, the prisoner had little choice but to agree to the surgery. "But please," he pleaded, "parachute my amputated limb back to my fatherland during your next bombing run." Overcome with sympathy and admiration for the prisoner's stoicism, the surgeon agreed to do the best he could to comply with this bizarre request, and the arm was indeed dropped over Berlin.

A little later, gangrene settled into the German officer's left leg. Again amputation was called for, again the prisoner made the same request, and again the American surgeon and a flight crew carried it out.

Finally the German's right foot had to come off too. The surgeon performed the operation and was in the process of attaching the severed limb to a parachute when the Polish chief rushed in. "Cease and desist!" he screamed. "Can't you see the man is trying to escape?"

•

A certain man had been going to a psychoanalyst for many years, and finally the doctor proclaimed him cured of his psychoses and mental debilities. On hearing the news, the ex-patient stood, shook the doctor's hand, and pulled out a revolver.

"What in God's name are you doing?" screamed the terrified shrink.

"You've helped me a great deal, Doctor," explained the man with a maniacal grin, "but now you know too much!"

•

A none-too-bright medical student who wished to go into neuropathology decided to conduct some research on the nervous system of the frog. Taking one out of the tank and placing it on the operating table, he yelled, "Jump!"

The frog jumped.

Taking his scalpel, the medical student amputated the frog's left front leg and yelled "Jump!"

The frog jumped.

He amputated a hind limb. "Jump!"

The frog produced a respectable hop.

Amputating a third limb, the student repeated his command. Gushing blood by now, the frog managed a feeble lurch.

Taking his scalpel to the fourth leg, he ordered the frog to jump. No response. "I said, *'Jump'!*" shouted the man. No response from the frog. The student bent over the table and bellowed *"JUMP!"* into the frog's ear. There was no movement from the animal whatsoever, so he decided to consider the experiment at an end.

Taking down his notebook, the medical student carefully noted his findings: "When all limbs are amputated, it has been determined that the frog goes deaf."

How can you spot a disadvantaged doctor?
  He's driving a domestic car.

•

How come you never see black people filling out
Organ Donor Cards?
  Because no one wants to end up with black lung.

•

This guy went to see his GP and was diagnosed
as having a tapeworm. "They're not easy to get rid
of, but we'll give it our best shot," the doctor told
him, and instructed him to come in every day for
two weeks, and to bring a lemon cookie and a
hard-boiled egg.
  The hapless sufferer agreed, and showed up next
morning with the two items. To his horror, the doctor shoved the hard-boiled egg up his asshole, followed it with the crumbled-up cookie, and sent
him home. This went on for twelve more days, at
which point the doctor's instructions were to forget
the cookie and to bring in the egg and a hammer.
  On the last day the fellow dropped his pants in
considerable apprehension, gritting his teeth as the

doctor inserted the egg up his ass and calmly sat back. A few minutes later the tapeworm stuck its head out and demanded, "Where the hell's my lemon cookie?"

And—*wham*—that was the end of the worm.

·

An extremely obese man showed up at the office of a famed nutritionist and claimed that he had tried every diet known to man, all to no avail. So the specialist proposed a radical approach: rectal feeding. "You'll be plenty hungry, but you won't starve," she reassured the desperate fatty, explaining that enough nutrients would be absorbed by the rectal walls to sustain life. "And you'll lose weight for sure."

After six weeks of scrupulously following the rectal regimen, the patient came in for a followup visit. Sure enough, he'd slimmed down from 312 pounds to a relatively trim 235. The doctor complimented him and went over to check his blood pressure, though she had a little trouble getting the cuff on because of the way his patient was energetically bouncing up and down in his seat.

"How're you feeling?" she asked, rather puzzled by this behavior.

"Great, Doc, never better," was the reply.

"In that case, do you mind explaining why you're bouncing up and down like that?"

"Oh, just chewing some gum!"

Did you hear about the prostitute who had an appendectomy?

The doctor sewed up the wrong hole, so now she's making money on the side.

•

The horny doctor always seemed to have a tough time persuading his wife to have sex, but one night he had a brainstorm. Just before climbing into bed, he handed her a glass of water and two aspirins.

"But Harvey, I don't have a headache," she whined.

"Gotcha!"

•

A nice girl finally screwed up her nerve and made an appointment with the famous Dr. O'Neal. She sat down in his office, blushed beet-red, and whispered, "Is it true you can make things grow, Dr. O'Neal?"

The doctor nodded reassuringly.

"Then please give me something to make my breasts grow," she blurted, clasping her hands over her nearly concave chest. "I can't bear being so flat-chested anymore."

"Easy enough," pronounced Dr. O'Neal. "You must say 'Mary had a little lamb' out loud three times a day."

The exhilarated young woman stopped at the supermarket on the way home. In the frozen-foods section she realized she was too excited to wait any longer, so she looked both ways and then said softly, "Mary had a little lamb."

Suddenly a man stepped out from the aisle behind her. "I see you've consulted Dr. O'Neal too," he said.

"Why yes," she stammered. "How did you know?"

Opening his fly and reaching in, he screamed, *"Hickory, dickory dock!"*

•

A mother and daughter lived together in devastating poverty, so it was cause for great rejoicing when the daughter found a dollar on the sidewalk on her way home from school. She ran home and showed it to her mother, who decided that for a dollar they could get a bottle of ketchup and two eggs and have themselves a real meal. So off went the daughter to the store.

As luck would have it, the little girl was happily skipping home when a truck backfired near her, startling her so much that she dropped the precious groceries. Staring down at the ruined feast, which lay smashed at her feet, the child burst into racking sobs.

"There, there, honey, don't cry," said an obstetrician who happened to be passing by. "It would've died anyway—its eyes were too far apart."

•

After a long and difficult delivery, the obstetrician finally pulled the baby out. Then he whirled it around over his head and let go, so that it splattered against the delivery room wall.

"Doctor!" screamed the woman, "that was my baby!!"

"Don't worry—it was dead anyhow."

•

Did you hear about the Pole who took his pregnant wife to the Chinese restaurant when she went into labor?

He'd heard they had free delivery.

•

Did you hear they found a cure for sickle-cell anemia?

The ink on a welfare check.

•

Did you hear about the new hospital for homosexuals under construction outside Atlanta?

It's called "Sick Fags Over Georgia."

•

If you get malaria from mosquitoes, and elephantiasis from tsetse flies, how do you get AIDS?

From the asshopper!

•

A state psychiatrist was touring an insane asylum and was very impressed with its rehabilitative program. In the first room he visited, an inmate was dexterously dribbling a basketball around the small space with astonishing skill, and shooting basket after basket into his wastebasket. "Most impressive, young man," praised the visitor.

"Thanks, Doc," said the athlete with a smile.

"When I get out of this joint I'm going to be a star with the New York Knicks!"

In the next room the psychiatrist found a patient engrossed by a pitching machine, and he was batting a solid .380. "Not bad," commented the doctor with a smile.

"I'm trying out for the Mets when I get out of here!" the baseball player announced confidently, clearly optimistic about his chances.

The scenario in the third room was puzzling, however. Looking through the window, the psychiatrist observed what seemed to be a patient humping a large burlap sack marked "Pecans."

"Good morning, young man," said the doctor, introducing himself. "Can you tell me what you're doing and about your plans for the future?"

"Isn't it obvious, Doctor?" asked the inmate, looking up with a wry grin. "I'm fuckin' nuts, and I'm never getting out of here."

•

Heard about the new non-profit institution called AMD?

It's "Mothers Against Dyslexia."

•

How many paranoid schizophrenics does it take to screw in a light bulb?
Who wants to know?

•

How come no neurosurgeons have leprosy?
They'd go to pieces under pressure.

•

Why couldn't the leper cross the road?
He didn't have the balls.

•

A bear walked into a bar in Butte, Montana, and was pissed off when the bartender refused to serve him a beer. "Why not?" growled the bear.
"Well, we don't serve beer to bears in Butte," explained the bartender.
"Okay, then get me a double Stoly on the rocks," ordered the bear.
"Nope. We don't serve booze to bears in Butte."
Really upset about the whole thing, the bear threatened to eat the woman sitting at the end of the bar. This had no effect on the bartender, so the

bear made good on his threat and devoured the woman. Walking back to the bartender, he ordered a beer to wash his meal down.

"Sorry," the bartender told the bear, "we don't serve drug addicts."

"And just who's the drug addict here?" demanded the bear.

"You are. That was a bar bitch you ate."

•

The waitress had scheduled an appointment after work with her gynecologist, and the doctor was quite taken aback when he came across a tea bag.

"Oh shit," said the waitress when the doctor held it up for her examination. "I wonder what I served my last customer . . ."

•

Definition of henpecked:
A sterile husband afraid to tell his pregnant wife.

•

After a few years of marriage the young woman became increasingly dismayed by her diminishing sex life. She tried everything she could think of, from greeting her husband at the door dressed in Saran Wrap to purchasing exotic paraphernalia from a mail-order sex boutique. But none of it had the desired effect on her husband's libido, and finally she persuaded him to consult a psychotherapist who'd had remarkable success treating sexual dysfunction via hypnotism.

She was delighted that after only a few visits, her husband's ardor was restored to honeymoon dimensions. There was only one annoying side effect: every so often during lovemaking he would jump up and run out of the room for a minute or two. At first his wife didn't want to rock the boat, but eventually her curiosity overcame her better judgement. Following him into the bathroom, she saw him staring into the mirror, muttering, "She's not my wife. . . . She's _not my wife_. . . . She's not my wife. . . ."

•

Soon after their honeymoon, the young couple found themselves at the doctor's office, where each complained of exhaustion and fatigue. After examining them thoroughly, the doctor reassured them that there was no organic reason for their complaints.

"However, it's not at all uncommon for young people to wear themselves out in the first weeks or months of married life," he reassured them. "What you both need is rest. So for the next month, confine your sexual activity to those days of the week

53

with an 'r' in them. That's Thursday, Friday, and Saturday," he went on with a wink, "and you'll be feeling up to snuff very soon."

Since the end of the week was approaching, the couple had no problem following the doctor's advice. But after only one scheduled night off, the new bride found herself increasingly restless and horny. Tossing and turning into the wee hours, she finally turned to her husband and shook him awake.

Groggy and bewildered, he mumbled, "What's wrong, baby? What day is it?"

"Mondray," she murmured.

•

As he got into bed the husband was very much in the mood, but was hardly surprised when his wife pushed his hand off her breast. "Lay off, honey. I have a headache."

"Perfect," he responded, without missing a beat. "I was just in the bathroom powdering my dick with aspirin."

•

Little Julie was the apple of her doctor father's eye, especially since she had been born with a heart condition and had always required pampering and special care. When she announced her engagement, Julie's father took it kind of hard, and on the wedding day he took the groom aside for a little talk.

"Listen, I don't know if Julie's told you this," he revealed, "but my little girl's awfully delicate. I think you ought to know that she has acute angina."

"Boy, that's good," said the groom with a grin, "because she sure doesn't have any tits!"

•

What do women and Tylenol have in common?

They're dangerous to mess with if someone else has broken the safety seal.

•

"I've been married three times and I'm still a virgin," complained Myrna to her new friend. "My first husband was a college professor; he only talked about it. My second husband was a doctor; he only looked at it. And my third husband was a gourmet."

•

"Doctor," the man told his physician, "I need a new penis."

The doctor took the request completely in stride. "No problem," he told his patient. "We have a five-incher, a seven-and-a-half-inch model, and a nine-incher. Which do you think would be right for you?"

"The nine-incher," the patient decided on the spot. "But would it be possible to take a look at it first?"

"Of course," said the doctor obligingly.

"Gee, Doctor," wondered the patient after a few moments, "isn't it available in white?"

•

What do you give to the man who has everything?
Penicillin.

•

The newly divorced forty-five-year-old made an appointment with a urologist and told him he wanted to be circumcised. "Most women seem to prefer it," he explained, "and now that I'm dating quite a bit I'd rather not worry about it."

The arrangements were made, and when the patient woke up from the surgery he saw the doctor standing by the bed with a very contrite expression on his face. "I've got good news and bad news," he admitted. "The bad news is that the knife slipped."

"Oh my God," gasped the patient. "What the hell's the good news?"

"Your dick wasn't malignant!"

•

Freddy's parents were both doctors, and worked such long hours that they had barely any time to spend with their son. So they were delighted when the chemistry set he'd been given for Christmas turned out to be a big hit. Freddy promptly disappeared with it into the basement.

Eventually, feeling guilty, his father found the time to came down to see how he was doing. He found Freddy, surrounded by test tubes, pounding away at the wall. "Son, why're you hammering a nail into the wall?" he asked.

"That's no nail, that's a worm," explained Freddy, and showed his dad the mixture in which he'd soaked the worm.

"Tell you what, pal," suggested Freddy's father, his eyes lighting up. "Lend me that test tube and I'll buy you a Toyota."

Needless to say, Freddy handed it over, and the next day when he got home from school he spotted a brand-new Mercedes Benz in the driveway. "Hey, Dad, what's up?" he called, running into the house.

"The Toyota's in the garage," explained his father, "and the Mercedes is from your Mom."

Sam wasn't happy about putting his dad in the state nursing home but it was all he could afford—until a lucky investment paid off. The first thing he did with his newfound wealth was to move his father to the fanciest retirement home in the whole state.

The old man was astounded by the luxury of his new surroundings and the attentiveness of the staff. On the first day, he started to list to his right side in front of the television. Instantly a nurse ran over and tactfully straightened him out. Over dinner he started to lean a bit to the left, but within a few seconds a nurse gently pushed him upright again.

That night his son called. "How're you doing, Pop?" he asked eagerly.

"Oh Sam, it's a wonderful place," said the father. "I've got my own color TV, the food is cooked by a French chef, the gardens look like Versailles, you wouldn't believe."

"Dad, it sounds perfect."

"There's one problem with the place, though, Sammy," the old fellow whispered. "They won't let you fart."

•

Ellen and Dan had been married for fifty-seven years when her health began to fail. Eventually she was hospitalized, and within a few weeks it became evident that she had only a few more days to live. "Dan, I have only one last request," she whispered to her husband with the last of her strength.

"Anything, dearest," her husband offered tenderly.

"In all those years we never had oral sex, and I don't want to die without knowing what it feels like. Go down on me."

Dan was more than a little taken aback, but he figured he'd gotten off easy all those years. So he proceeded to close the door and comply with his wife's dying wish.

He was even more startled to observe a distinct blush on her cheeks the next day at what he expected would be his final visit. To Dan's amazement and that of the whole hospital, Ellen was sitting up in bed the following day, and within a week she was well enough to be discharged.

Dan was in the room when the doctor told them the happy news, and Ellen was shocked to see her husband break down in tears. "Dan, what's wrong? What's wrong?" she implored.

"I was just realizing," sobbed Dan, "that I could have saved Eleanor Roosevelt."

•

The well-meaning psychologist was seeing if Mrs. Englehardt qualified for admission to the local nursing home, and part of the standard procedure was a test for senility. "And what's this?" she asked sweetly of the old German woman, who was sitting at the dinner table.

"Dot? Dot's a spoon," answered Mrs. Englehardt.

"Very good," said the doctor. "And this?"

"Dot's a fork," answered the old woman.

"*Very* good. And this?" asked the social worker, holding up a knife.

"Dot's a phallic symbol."

•

"Yeah, Doc, what's the news?" answered Fred when his doctor called with his test results.

"I have some bad news and some really bad news," admitted the doctor. "The bad news is that you only have twenty-four hours to live."

"Oh my God," gasped Fred, sinking to his knees. "What could be worse news than that?"

"I couldn't get hold of you yesterday."

•

Thoroughly fed up with his wife's incessant bitching and moaning, Joe finally agreed to accompany her to a meeting with her therapist. Once there, he made his reluctance quite clear, along with the fact that he had no idea how she found so much to complain about all the time.

"Well, Mr. Johnson," the therapist pointed out gently, "it *is* customary for married people to have sexual intercourse regularly, even frequently. Mrs. Johnson tells me that even on the nights when you don't fall asleep in front of the TV, you never respond in any way to her sexual advances."

"Yeah, well, so?" Joe scratched his head. "So whaddaya recommend?"

"Well, a reasonable minimum might be sexual intercourse at least twice a week," suggested the counselor.

"Twice a week, huh?" grunted Joe, thinking it over. "Okay, I could drop her off on Mondays—but on Fridays she's gotta take the bus."

•

When Mike showed up for his appointment with the urologist, the doctor informed him a sperm sample was necessary, and instructed him to go to Room Four. Dutifully going down the hall, Mike opened the door to Room Four and found two absolutely gorgeous women clad in scanty lingerie. They proceeded to arouse him beyond his wildest dreams, and Mike headed back down the hall with a dreamy smile and a *terrific* sperm sample.

Realizing he had to pee, Mike opened the door to the first bathroom he came across, only to interrupt a guy frantically beating off with a copy of *Hustler.* In the second bathroom a fellow was busy masturbating with the company of the *Penthouse* centerfold. Back in the doctor's office and curious as hell, Mike couldn't resist asking the doctor about the other two fellows.

"Oh, them?" sniffed the doctor dismissively. "Those're my Medicaid patients."

•

What did the man in the shower die of?
Poison Ivory.

•

Visiting New York City for a medical convention, a doctor from the University of Utah took the afternoon off to do some shopping. Wandering into a little antique store, he came across a curious brass sculpture of a rat and inquired as to the price. "I have to tell you the truth," said the proprietor. "I've sold that piece twice and it's been returned twice—so I'll let you have it for $400. It's very old."

The doctor paid and headed out with his purchase in a bag under his arm. Not much later he noticed the shadowy forms of hundreds of live rats scuttling along in the gutters. A little while later the rats had swelled in number to several thousand, and it became evident they were following the doctor. His astonishment turned to disgust and alarm as the rat pack grew to fill up the whole street, so he picked up speed and headed east. When he reached the river, he chucked the brass rat right in, and to his considerable relief the horde of rats followed it to a watery death.

The next morning the doctor was the very first customer in the antique store.

"No way, buddy, I'm not taking it back a third time," protested the owner.

"Relax, I'm not bringing the rat back," soothed the doctor. "I just wanted to know . . . do you have a brass lawyer?"

•

Why didn't the skeleton cross the road?
He didn't have the guts.

•

When Jack was born, his mother called out, "What is it Doctor, a boy or a girl?"

"Got me," admitted the doctor. "I can't get it off the wall."

•

The construction worker rushed over to the scene of an accident and pulled a heavy beam off a woman lying on the sidewalk.

"Hang in there lady," he urged, taking her hand. "Are you badly hurt?"

"How should I know?" she snapped. "I'm a doctor, not a lawyer!"

•

"Tell me about you and your husband's love life," suggested the shrink.

"Well, it's like the Fourth of July," said the woman after a moment's reflection.

"Aha—you mean it's all firecrackers and emotional explosions?" pursued the doctor eagerly.

"No, no. I mean it happens once a year."

•

Lawyer: "Are you sure you can prove to the satisfaction of the court that my client is insane?"

Doctor: "No problem. And if you ever need it, I'll be glad to do the same for you."

•

Mike was touching up the paint in the bathroom one weekend when the brush slipped out of his hand, leaving a stripe across the toilet seat. So Mike painted the whole seat over, and then went off to a ball game.

His wife happened to get home early, went up-stairs to pee, and found herself firmly stuck to the toilet seat. At four o'clock Mike found her there, furious and embarrassed, but was unable to dis-lodge her for fear of tearing the skin.

With considerable difficulty Mike managed to get her into the back seat of the car and then into a wheelchair at the county hospital, where she was wheeled into a room and maneuvered, on her knees, onto an examining table. At this point the resident entered and surveyed the scene. "What do you think, Doc?" broke in the nervous husband.

"Nice, very nice," he commented, stroking his chin. "But why the cheap frame?"

•

Then there was the doctor who gave one of his patients two months to live. When he found out she couldn't pay the bill, he gave her another three months.

•

When Alec was informed by his doctor that he had only twelve more hours to live, he rushed home and told his wife, who collapsed in racking sobs. But then she pulled herself together, clasped his hands in hers, and promised, "Then I'm going to make tonight the best night of your life, darling." She went out and bought all his favorite delicacies, opened a bottle of fine champagne, served him dinner dressed in his favorite sexy peignoir, and led him up to bed, where she made passionate love to him.

Just as they were about to fall asleep, Alec tapped her on the shoulder. "Honey, could we make love again?"

"Sure, sweetheart," she said sleepily, and obliged.

"Once more, baby?" he asked afterwards. "It's our last night together."

"Mmmhmm," she mumbled, and they made love a third time.

"One last time, darling," he begged a little later, shaking her by the shoulders.

"Fine!" she snapped. "After all, what do you care? *You* don't have to get up in the morning!"

•

A doctor had been working insane hours, spending twelve and fourteen hours a day at the hospital, six or seven days a week. Finally he turned to a fellow surgeon and declared, "That's it—I'm going home for the weekend so my kids will remember what I look like."

"Just keep an eye on who *they* look like," his co-worker advised.

•

How many doctors does it take to change a light bulb?

It depends on what kind of insurance the bulb has.

•

Ralph was a little embarrassed, but he said bluntly, "Doctor, I can't take a shit."

The doctor assured him that constipation was a common problem, and wrote out a prescription. "Take one tablespoon three times a day, and call me if the problem persists into next week."

A week later, Ralph was on the phone complaining that his bowels still had not moved.

"Hmmm," mused the doctor. "I'll telephone in a prescription to your pharmacy for some pills. One every four hours should fix you right up, but come in next week if you're still experiencing problems."

After a week had gone by, Ralph came into the office. "This is really flipping me out, Doc—the pills haven't had any effect at all, and I've been taking them every four hours, just like you said."

"Obviously this case is more intractable than I thought," the physician admitted, "and I'd better get a complete history. I have your name; where do you live?" Ralph told him. "And your occupation?"

"I'm a musician."

"Aha," cried the doctor, brightening and reaching for her purse. "Why didn't you say so in the first place? Here's some money so you can go buy some *food.*"

Freddie was thrilled when he graduated from medical school. "What a profession," he chortled to an old buddy. "You can order women to strip naked, look 'em over inside and out—and then send a bill to their husbands."

•

There was considerable jealousy surrounding Dr. Atkinson, who not only had a lucrative practice, a luxurious home, and a Bentley, but also a telephone in the Bentley.

A fellow plastic surgeon decided not to be one-upped by Atkinson, so he had a phone installed in his Porsche. And the first call he placed was to Atkinson. "George," he said, "I just want you to know you're not the only doctor in L.A. who can afford a phone in his car."

"Hang on a sec, would you Phil?" interrupted Atkinson. "I've got another call."

•

"Doctor, Doctor," screamed the frantic young mother, "my baby just ate an entire tube of K-Y jelly! What should we do?"

Holding the receiver away from his ear, the doctor thought for a moment, then counseled, "Well, if you really can't wait, Parcells Drug is open all night."

•

Hear the one about the lovesick gynecologist who looked up an old girlfriend . . . ?

•

"Dr. Merrill," shrieked the nurse receptionist, bursting into his office. "You pronounced Mr. Van Heusen as healthy as a bull, and he just dropped dead outside the front door."

"Quick, Felice," ordered the doctor without missing a beat, "turn him around so it looks like he was coming *in.*"

•

Mrs. Friedrich could hardly believe it when her hard-driving husband finally agreed to take a week off and take his wife and daughter to the Caribbean. As they lazed on the beach on their first afternoon, she decided to bring up something that had been bothering her. "You know, David, I understand that as the head of the cardiology department you're under a lot of pressure, that you have to make sure a lot of people under you do their jobs, observe correct procedures, every minute of the day," she began sympathetically.

"Damn straight."

"But family life isn't exactly the same situation," she proceeded cautiously, "and sometimes I think you're a little too strict with little Wendy."

"That's absurd," blustered Dr. Friedrich, watching as his five-year-old daughter ran happily into the surf. Jumping to his feet, he yelled, "Wendy, get back here this minute! You're tracking sand into the ocean!"

•

At the seminar on psychopathology and its implications for the judicial system, a lawyer listened closely to the eminent psychiatrist's lecture. Finally he raised his hand and pointed out, "You've been telling us a great deal about the abnormal person, about pathological states and related behavior. But what happens if my client is normal?"

"Not to worry," assured the doctor. "If we ever come across someone like that, we'll cure him too."

•

Late one night a young man ran into the corner pharmacy and up to the pharmacist. "Do you know any way to stop hiccups?" he asked anxiously.

Without any warning, the pharmacist gave him a terrific slap in the face. Ignoring the fellow's shock and dismay, he pointed out brightly, "See—you don't have the hiccups anymore, now do you?"

"No," replied the man, ruefully rubbing his cheek, "but my girlfriend out in the car still does."

•

"Which side is it best to lie on, Doctor?" asked the lawyer at the cocktail party, eager for some free medical advice.

The doctor answered sagely, "The side that pays you the retainer."

•

Following Thomson's physical, Dr. Munro sent his patient a bill. When a month went by without a remittance, Munro sent another bill, and then another, and then another, but to no avail. Finally, he sent Thomson a pathetic letter, claiming desperately straightened circumstances and enclosing a picture of his infant daughter. On the back of the snapshot, he wrote, "The reason I need the money you owe me."

Barely a week later a response from Thomson

arrived in the mail. Munro ripped it open eagerly, and found himself holding a picture of a gorgeous woman in a mink coat. On the back of the photograph, his patient had scrawled, "The reason I can't pay."

•

At a dinner party an attorney found herself seated next to a doctor, and they got to discussing the nuisance of constantly being approached for free professional advice during social situations. "I never know how to handle it gracefully," she admitted. "Got any advice?"

"I don't know if this'll work for you," said the doctor, "but I stop them cold with one word: 'undress.'"

•

Bert had just turned fifty and became concerned that his stamina in bed was really declining. So he went to consult his doctor, who pointed out that his general physical condition left something to be desired. "You're a little overweight, you're easily winded, you're just out of shape. I recommend jogging five miles a day," said the doctor. "It'll really improve your stamina in general." And though Bert was a couch potato by nature, he reluctantly agreed to the regimen.

A week later, the phone rang. "Hi Bert, how're you feeling?" asked the doctor.

"Really terrific," enthused his patient.

"And how's your sex life?"

"What sex life?" countered Bert. "I'm thirty-five miles from home."

•

The story goes that a doctor friend of Clarence Darrow once tried to persuade him that he should have chosen a medical career. When Darrow said he saw nothing wrong with practicing law, his friend argued back. "It's not to say that all lawyers are dishonest, but you must admit that your profession doesn't exactly make angels out of men."

"True enough," Darrow readily conceded. "In that regard you doctors certainly have the best of us."

•

Nate was in a nasty accident, and broke so many bones that it was necessary for him to be placed in a body cast, with all four limbs and his neck immobilized in traction. And during his lengthy hospitalization, he had to be fed rectally.

The attending nurse felt especially sorry for him when his birthday came around, so she decided to give him a special treat: some ice cream through the food tube. But she'd barely left the room before Nate's screams of "Nurse! Nurse!" echoed down the corridor.

Rushing back in, she cried, "What's the matter? Is it too cold? I'm so sorry—"

"No, no, no," Nate howled back. "I *hate* rum raisin!"

•

What's the difference between a doctor and a lawyer?

When a case is over, the lawyer asks himself, "Did I leave anything out?" and the doctor asks himself, "Did I leave anything in?"

•

"I hope I'm sick, I hope I'm sick, I hope I'm sick," muttered the dejected man sitting across from Doreen in the doctor's waiting room. Finally she could no longer restrain her curiosity, and asked, "Excuse me, but why are you hoping you're sick?"

The man peered up at her dimly and explained, "I'd hate to be well and feel like this."

•

Have you seen the new home surgery kit available via mail order?

It's called Suture Self.

•

After examining the young woman, the doctor handed her a prescription. "Take one of these after every meal," she instructed.

"But Doctor," she protested, "like I told you, I haven't been able to eat for three and a half days."

"So look on the bright side—the medication will last longer."

•

When Dr. Cortez ran into a patient on the street, he cleared his throat, and said, "Uh, Miss Porter . . . that check you sent me a few months ago never cleared."

"Is that so?" she retorted. "Neither did my arthritis."

•

At the monthly staff meeting, the hospital director brought up the head nurse's accusation that Dr.

Stone had addressed her in a rude and vulgar manner. "We must censure this sort of behavior," the chief pointed out. "Have you anything to say in your defense?"

"Let me explain the extenuating circumstances," requested Dr. Stone. "First of all, my alarm didn't go off. So when I saw how late I was I jumped out of bed, caught my foot in the sheets and fell over, smacking my head into the bedside table and breaking the lamp. As I was shaving the doorbell rang, and I cut myself. It was a young fellow selling encyclopedias, and I had to buy A through G before I could get rid of him. I'd forgotten my bagel in the toaster oven, so it was burnt and my coffee was cold. On my way to the car I slipped, bruising my knee and tearing my coat, and then the battery turned out to be dead. It took forty-five minutes for the serviceman to come over and get the car started. I should have taken a cab anyway, because in the hospital parking lot the snowplow smashed into the car, totalling the front end."

Dr. Stone took a deep breath and continued. "And when I finally got up to my office and sat down at my desk to collect myself, Nurse McMahon burst in and said, 'Doctor, that shipment of six dozen thermometers just arrived—where do you want me to put them?'"

.

Then there's the story of the elderly Italian gent who came in to see his doctor. He explained that he was thinking of marrying a considerably younger woman, and wanted the doctor's opinion as to whether he was sexually fit.

"Okay," agreed the doctor. "Let's have a look at your sexual organs."

"Here they are," said the old man, and obligingly stuck out his index finger and tongue.

•

An idealistic young doctor decided to serve the less fortunate, so he volunteered for the Peace Corps. He was put in charge of a population-control program in a remote Nepalese hill town. It turned out to be impossible for the women to keep track of birth-control pills, so the doctor decided to concentrate on the use of condoms.

His first patient was a man whose wife had given birth to six children in as many years, and neither wanted more. The doctor explained how the sheaths worked, and that if he wore one conscientiously, his wife would not get pregnant. So he was surprised when the fellow's wife came in a month later, and found she was pregnant again.

"What happened?" he scolded. "All your husband had to do was keep the condom on—is that so difficult?"

"He try, he try very hard," stammered the poor woman, "but after three days he have to pee so bad he cut the end off."

•

"Come on, Mr. Bergland," coaxed the dentist, "open wider. Wider. A little wider . . ."

"Look, Doctor," Bergland broke in, "if you're going to climb in, I'll get out of the way."

•

When the two specialists were called in for a bedside consultation, each slipped his hand under the covers, where they accidentally grasped each other's wrists and felt for a pulse.

One nodded gravely and murmured, "Rheumatic fever."

The other shook his head. "She's just drunk."

•

McMurtry put off going to the dentist for so long that most of his teeth had fallen out, but he could finally postpone no longer. When the dentist had inspected his mouth, McMurtry's worst fears were confirmed: he needed to have the remaining teeth extracted and a complete set of dentures made up. "You'll have a dazzling smile again, you'll be able to eat corn on the cob—it'll be wonderful, you'll be thrilled," the dentist assured him.

Sweat beaded up on McMurtry's brow at the prospect. "You don't understand," he whispered. "I'm terrified of pain."

"Pain? What pain? You won't feel a thing." His

patient was not persuaded, so the dentist had an idea. "Tell you what," he proposed. "I just performed the same procedure on a guy named Felix Katz. Why don't you call him up right now? He'll tell you the truth—he felt no pain whatsoever." He dialed the number and handed it over.

After he'd introduced himself and confirmed that he was indeed speaking to the correct Felix Katz, McMurtry pleaded, "Tell me the truth, Mr. Katz. Did it hurt? Yes or no?"

"Yes or no, I can't quite say," answered Katz, "but I can tell you about no pain. Our dentist finished with me in February and now it's June, right? A perfect day for doing a little work on the house, so I'm up on a ladder checking the gutters when I lose my balance. I land on a sawhorse, right on my nuts. And would you believe it, Mr. McMurtry—it was the first time in five months that my teeth didn't hurt!"

•

Two psychiatrists met at a medical convention and were comparing notes on their toughest cases. "Mine was this fellow with delusions of grandeur," said Sharpe. "He told everyone that he stood to inherit the oil rights to half of Texas and a diamond mine in South Africa, claimed that he was just waiting for the deeds to come in the mail. It took me four years of bi-weekly sessions to get his feet on the ground."

"So?" pursued his colleague.

"So just when I had him cured, the damn letter arrived."

•

The nervous mother put in an urgent call to her son's pediatrician. "Tell me, Dr. Coffey," she asked, "is it true that certain vegetables can actually stop a child from growing?"

The pediatrician reflected for a moment and then replied, "I suppose so, but it depends on where you put them."

•

The young Irish bride made her first appointment with a gynecologist and told him of her and her husband's wish to start a family. "We've been trying for months now, Dr. Rizzoli, and I don't seem to be able to get pregnant," she confessed miserably.

"I'm sure we'll solve the problem," the doctor reassured her. "If you'll just get up on the examining table and take off your underpants . . ."

"Well, all right, Doctor," agreed the young woman, blushing, "but I'd rather have my husband's baby."

•

Three college roommates got together regularly over the years, even though their professional lives differed widely: one had become an attorney, one a professor of Italian literature, and one a zoologist. When next they met up, they made a pretty gloomy trio, and it turned out that each had been told by his physician that he had only six months to live. Understandably, the conversation turned to the way in which each intended to live out his remaining days.

"I'm going to Rwanda in Africa," decided the zoologist. "I've always wanted to see the mountain gorilla in its native habitat."

"Italy for me. I want to walk where Dante walked, to be buried near the great man. And you?" asked the professor, turning to the third friend. "What would you like to see?"

"Another doctor," said the lawyer.

•

Did you hear about the plastic surgeon who thought his dick was too small?

He decided to hang himself.

•

This was Eckendorf's first visit to the eminent renologist, and Dr. Stern was taking down his medical history. "And whom have you consulted about your condition before coming to me?" asked the great doctor.

"Only the pharmacist at Bigelow's," replied Eckendorf rather sheepishly.

Stern made no effort to conceal his contempt for the sort of advice available from those who dispensed medical advice without a license to do so. "Idiots like that cretin only aggravate most conditions," he ranted. "And what sort of absurd recommendations did that ignoramus come up with?"

"He told me to come see you."

•

Miss Horn was grotesquely overweight, so her doctor finally prescribed a strict regimen, telling her it was the only way to avoid serious health problems in the future. "I want you to eat normally for two days, but then skip a day, drinking only water. Repeat this three times, and by the time I see you next Thursday you'll have lost at least six pounds."

The patient promised to obey, and indeed when she showed up for the appointment she was almost twenty pounds lighter.

"Excellent progress, Miss Horn," enthused the doctor, quite amazed. "And you lost all this weight simply by following my instructions?"

Miss Horn nodded. "It wasn't easy, though, Doctor," she admitted. "On that third day, I felt like I was about to die."

"From hunger, eh?" The doctor clucked sympathetically.

"No, no," she explained, "from skipping."

•

The psychiatrist paid close attention as his new client described the situation that was causing him so much anxiety. Afterwards, the psychiatrist confidently told him that it really didn't seem to be a terribly incapacitating problem. "Frankly, Mr. Bach," he said reassuringly, "I've known many, many men who prefer boxer shorts to Jockey-type briefs. In fact, I'm one of them."

"Is that so?" A smile came over Bach's face as he leaned over and eagerly pursued the matter. "And do you like them with French dressing or Thousand Island?"

•

McCain was outraged when his dentist's bill arrived in the mail, and lost no time reaching the office by phone. "It was just a simple extraction," he complained bitterly, "but you've charged me three times your normal rate."

"I had to," explained the dentist. "You made so much noise two patients ran out of the waiting room."

"Note the deformation of the joints due to rheumatic arthritis," lectured the medical school professor, waving his pointer at the illuminated X-ray. "In addition, this patient limps because of damage to the right tibia—note the pronounced curvature—sustained in an industrial accident." Turning to the roomful of aspiring radiologists, the professor asked, "Now tell me, in a case like this, what would you do?"

Johannsen stuck up his hand. "Well, sir," he offered, "I bet I'd limp too."

•

What's the fastest way to make a million dollars? Become a plastic surgeon and work part-time.

•

Orville went to specialist after specialist in search of a diagnosis, and it finally emerged that he was suffering from a rare enzymatic disorder, the only treatment for which was fresh breast milk. So he advertised in the want ads for a wet nurse, and was delighted when a woman promptly responded. Explaining the situation over the phone, he negotiated a price and made an appointment for the next day.

It happened that Orville had always been a tit man and had an exceptionally skilled set of lips and tongue, and that after a few minutes the woman found herself extremely aroused. Squirming, and breathing heavily, she managed to gasp, "Uh . . . is there anything else I could offer you?"

"Mmm," murmured Orville, looking up and licking his lips. "You don't happen to have any Oreos, do you?"

•

Although she was an internist, Dr. Henderson learned more than a little practical psychology over his years in practice. Observing that the sleepless Mrs. Rosenkrantz bothered the hospital staff all night long, yet refused to take her sedatives, she made sure to stand just outside her room when she instructed the night nurse to give her an enema when she next awoke.

Mrs. Rosenkrantz slept for three days.

•

"So tell me, Mr. Duffy," asked the young intern, eager to practice his bedside manner, "do you suffer from hemorrhoids?"

"Such an idiot—and you're gonna be a doctor?" marveled Duffy. "What *else* can you do with 'em?"

•

What's the scariest thing about flu season?
When you describe your symptoms to the doctor and he starts backing away from you.

•

Tim and Elaine decided to tie the knot, and went to the doctor for the requisite physical exams. Afterwards the doctor called Tim into his office and told him he had some good news and some bad news. "The good news," he explained, "is that your fiancée has gonorrhea."

Tim paled. "If that's the *good* news, Doctor, then what the hell's next?"

The doctor elaborated. "Tim, the bad news is that she didn't get it from you."

•

Hear about the gynecologist who started going to an analyst . . .
. . . because he was always feeling low?

When Robinson stretched out on the psychiatrist's couch, he was clearly in a bad state. "Doctor," he pleaded, voice quavering and hands twitching, "you've got to help me. I really think I'm losing my mind. I have no memory of what happened to me a year ago, nor even of a few weeks back. I can't even recall yesterday with any clarity. I can't cope with daily life—in fact, I think I'm going insane."

"Keep calm, Mr. Robinson," soothed the shrink. "I'm sure I'll be able to help you. Now tell me: how long have you had this problem?"

Robinson looked up blankly. "What problem?"

●

Definition of a family doctor:
He treats your family, you support his.

●

The psychiatrist closed his notebook, clasped his hands in satisfaction, and contemplated the patient sitting across from him. "I confess that in my profession one seldom speaks of 'cures,' Miss Kamin," he said sagely, "but at this time I am very pleased to be able to pronounce you one-hundred percent cured. Good-bye, and good luck."

"Swell," muttered the woman, looking downcast and beginning to pout. "That's just swell."

The psychiatrist was taken by surprise. "Miss Kamin, I thought you'd be delighted. What on earth is wrong?"

"Oh, it's fine for you," snapped Miss Kamin, "but look at it from my side. Three years ago I was Joan of Arc. Now I'm nobody."

•

When Roger met Ruby in a bar one night, he thought she was gorgeous, and he remained intrigued even after she'd confessed to having an incredible foot fetish. So he accepted her invitation to come back to her place, and obligingly fucked her with his big toe.

A few days later he woke up with his toe swollen and throbbing. He hobbled over to the doctor, where he was told he had syphillis of the foot. Roger admitted he'd never known such a condition existed. "Is it rare, Doc?"

"Fairly, but I've seen weirder," the doctor told him. "Just this morning a lady came in with athlete's cunt."

•

"I think you better sit down," said the doctor to the handsome young man about town. "I've gotten your test results back, and I have some terrible news."

"What, Doctor, what?" gasped Mark.

The doctor took a deep breath. "Mark, you have a rare and incurable blood disorder that will kill you in six months or less."

"Six months!" screeched the young man, understandably panicked. "What should I do, Dr. Bergland, what in God's name should I do?"

The doctor considered the question for a few moments, then shrugged. "If I were in your shoes, I'd marry an ugly woman and move to Kansas. It'll be the longest six months of your life."

•

When the teenager went to the urologist complaining of discharge dripping from his penis, the doctor took one look and told him he had V.D.

"No way," protested the young man with a blush. "It's gotta be a cold."

"Have it your way, sonny," said the urologist. "But we have to treat it like the clap until it sneezes."

•

How did the sympathetic doctor treat the kleptomaniac?

He gave her something to take.

•

The doctor's wife was awakened out of a sound sleep by her husband frantically shaking her by the shoulders. "Honey, find my bag, please. I've got to dash—some guy just phoned and said he couldn't live without me!"

"Hang on, Barney, hang on," she mumbled. "I'm pretty sure that call was for me."

•

"Y'know, Candy," said the hooker to her roommate, "I'm afraid I'm going to quit going to therapy."

"Gee, how come, honey? I thought you said Dr. Wolverman was really helping you a lot."

"Oh, he is, he is . . . but I just can't get used to lying down for a guy and then having *him* bill *me*."

•

Did you hear about the resourceful proctologist?

He always used two fingers, in case his patients wanted a second opinion.

•

Aunt Jean was rattling along in her Oldsmobile when she got a flat tire. Being an independent sort, she jacked up the car and undid the nuts and bolts, but as she was pulling the tire off, she lost her balance and fell backwards onto the hubcap holding the hardware. And it rolled right down into a storm sewer.

This entire incident occurred right outside the state insane asylum and happened to be observed by an inmate watching carefully through the bars. "Listen, lady," he called out, "just use one bolt from each of the other three tires. They'll be plenty strong enough to get you to the gas station."

"Quick thinking," said Aunt Jean admiringly. "Now why on earth is a bright boy like you stuck in that place?"

"Lady, I'm here for being crazy, not stupid."

•

Tires squealing, the frantic man screeched to a halt in front of the drugstore and ran inside. "You gave my wife cyanide instead of a bromide!" he screamed.

"That's terrible," replied the druggist. "And you owe me another $8.50."

•

The young man made an appointment with the sex therapist and admitted that he and his wife's sex life had gone completely to pot. "We've only been married three years, but all the romance is gone. The only way I can imagine perking things up is by having an affair."

The therapist was quick to dissuade him from such a rash solution. "Instead of taking such a terrible risk, try bringing a little creativity to your sex life. How about making love at a different time of day, or maybe somewhere you've never done it before?" she suggested.

He was skeptical but agreed to give it a try, and sure enough he showed up for his next appointment with a big grin on his face. "You know, you were right, Doc," he admitted cheerfully. "I was having dinner with the little lady when we slipped our shoes off and started playing footsie, and pretty soon she had her panties off and my fly was open, and a few minutes later we were making love right on top of the table! It was the best sex we've ever had."

The therapist was delighted, and congratulated him on his inventiveness.

"There's one thing that bothers me, though," admitted the fellow, a shadow crossing his face.

"And what's that?" she asked kindly.

"I don't think we're ever going to get a seat in that Howard Johnson's again."

•

Things at the hospital started to calm down after 3 a.m. or so, so the resident on duty, realizing he was starving, headed for the greasy spoon across the street. The grumpy waitress standing by the booth scratched her ass as she waited for him to order.

Forgetting he was off-duty, the doctor inquired, "Do you have hemorrhoids?"

"Look, buddy, *no* special orders," she snapped.

•

Mrs. Garwood lived up in the hills and had always been as healthy as a horse, but as old age approached, she found herself suffering from some "female troubles." Finally she confessed this to her daughter-in-law, who made an appointment with a gynecologist in the city and drove her in.

A wide-eyed Mrs. Garwood lay silent and still as a stone while the doctor examined her. When it was over, she sat up and fixed a beady eye on the physician. "You seem like such a nice young man," she quavered. "But, tell me, does your mother know what you do for a living?"

When Harry started feeling tired and run-down, his doctor couldn't reach a satisfactory diagnosis, so he put Harry in the hospital for a battery of tests. After a day of being poked and prodded and pricked, Harry was exhausted, so when the nurse came in with some chicken noodle soup, he waved her away and dropped off to sleep.

In the meantime the first test results had come in, and Harry's doctor realized that his patient's lethargy was the result of nothing more than severe constipation. So he ordered the night nurse to administer an enema to the groggy patient without delay. The next morning he observed with satisfaction that all Harry's vital signs were much improved, and he discharged him with a slap on the back.

"So how was the hospital, honey?" asked Harry's wife on the drive home.

"Not too bad, I guess," he answered, "but I have a tip for you in case you're ever admitted: if they serve you soup, be sure to eat it."

"How come? You think the soup's what fixed you up?"

"Oh, no," said Harry, "but if you *don't* eat it, they make you take it up the ass."

Finally Mr. Garcia ran out of patience. "All these months I've been coming back to you for all those extra treatments, following all your instructions, buying your expensive medications and customized equipment, paying your exorbitant fees—why, you've made a king's ransom off me alone, and I don't feel one bit better. You're a charlatan, Dr. Ludlow. You're nothing but a quack!"

The physician clucked his tongue and shook his head sadly. "Gratitude," he sighed, "I suppose that's all the gratitude I can expect. And to think I named my yacht after you."

•

Every ten years or so, Maw and Paw would make the long trip from Beaver Creek to visit one or another of their children, and each time the exposure to television and magazines and newspapers gave them plenty to talk about for the next decade.

After one such trip, the old man was fit to be tied the whole way home.

"Why, what's got inta you, Paw?" asked his wife. "It's those durn scientists, isn't it? Are you riled about all the toxic waste bein' dumped on us country folk? Or has that pesky greenhouse effect got you upset?"

"Heck, no, Maw," he snorted. "It's that they're trying to sell something besides liquor to cure a cold."

•

What's the difference between herpes and true love?

Herpes lasts forever.

•

After carefully noting the family history, the psychiatrist turned to the older woman and asked gently, "Now Mrs. Herman, this eccentricity in your daughter, couldn't it be called hereditary?"

Mrs. Herman pulled herself up in her chair and retorted, "Let me set the record straight on that one, Doctor: there has *never* been anything hereditary on either side of the family!"

•

Millie Hawkes was pushing eighty-five, and her constipation finally became so acute that she made an appointment with an internist. "I've got it bad," she confessed. "My bowels haven't moved in over a week."

"I see," said the doctor, making a note on her chart. "And what do you do for it?"

"Well, I give it every opportunity, not that it seems to matter," she answered. "I sit in the bathroom for a good half an hour every morning, and almost that long after supper, too."

"That's not quite what I meant, Mrs. Hawkes,"

the doctor interrupted gently. "I mean, do you take anything?"

"Naturally," replied the old woman tartly. "I always take a book."

•

Terribly agitated, Jack rushed into his dentist's examining room and ushered the hygienist firmly to the door. Once he was alone with the doctor, he unzipped his fly and gingerly pulled out his dick.

"Jack, Jack," said the dentist, taken aback. "I'm a dentist. If you think you have V.D., you need to see your regular doctor."

"It's not V.D." gasped Jack, "and you've gotta help me. There's a tooth stuck in it."

•

After much soul-searching, and having determined the husband was infertile, the childless couple decided to try artificial insemination. So the woman made an appointment at the clinic, where she was told to undress from the waist down, get on the table, and place her feet in the gynecological stirrups. She was feeling rather awkward about the whole procedure, and when the doctor came in, her anxiety was not diminished by the sight of him pulling down his pants.

"Wait a minute! What the hell's going *on* here?" she yelped, pulling herself up to a sitting position.

"Don't you want to get pregnant?" asked the doctor breezily. "Well, we're out of the bottled stuff, so you'll have to settle for what's on tap."

•

"I just hope it's not Alzheimer's," confessed Lundqvist. "Maybe there's some kind of memory medicine you can give me. See, I'm getting terribly forgetful. I lose track of where I'm going or what I'm supposed to do when I get there. What should I do?" he asked glumly.

"Pay me in advance," the doctor promptly suggested.

•

"I must admit I was pretty puzzled by the results of this morning's urinalysis," said the doctor, "until I realized the bottle you gave me was full of apple juice instead of pee."

"Oh, no," gasped the woman, turning pale. "Doctor Hernandez, may I use your phone?"

"Of course . . . but why?" he asked, handing over the receiver.

"The other bottle must be in Brittany's lunch box!"

A tight-fisted Scot, Guthrie waited till his tooth was killing him before telephoning the dentist. "Tell me, what d'ye charge for extracting a molar?" he asked.

"Twenty-five pounds," was the reply.

"Twenty-five pounds!" Guthrie howled in outrage. "For a few minutes' work?"

"If you'd prefer, Mr. Guthrie," offered the obliging dentist, "I could reduce the cost and make it take considerably longer."

•

When Carl and Billy got the notices from the draft board, they decided anything was preferable to serving in Vietnam. So, to change their status from 1A to 4F, they had every tooth in their heads extracted.

On the day appointed for their physicals, they agreed to meet at the draft board good and early. Unfortunately, Billy was a little late, so a construction worker got between the two of them in line. He smelled as though he hadn't bathed since the Interstate had gone in three years before, and if he hadn't been bigger than a Frigidaire, both hippies would've held their noses.

Finally Carl's turn came. When he said he had no teeth, and the medic had felt in his mouth to see for himself, he pronounced him 4F and called out, "Next!"

"So what's wrong with you, buddy?" asked the doctor suspiciously of the giant construction worker.

"I got real bad piles," he grunted.

"Is that so? Bend over." The medic stuck his fingers up the guy's ass, then stood up and confirmed, "4F. Next!"

Billy stepped up and looked miserably at the medic's shit-covered finger as the guy barked, "And what's wrong with you, pal?"

"Nothing," he mumbled. "Absolutely nothing."

•

The two psychiatrists were sharing an elevator at the end of the day. "I've got to hand it to you, Feldstein," said Goldberg admiringly. "All day long you listen to people's miseries and anxieties, but you always look fresh as a daisy. How do you do it?"

Feldstein shrugged. "Who listens?"

•

Oliver was pretty nervous about going under the knife, and when he woke up his worst fears were realized: besides the big bandage over his belly, his groin was swathed in gauze. He yelled for the nurse, who summoned the doctor, who hastened to assure him that the stomach surgery had been a complete success.

"Why the hell am I bandaged down there, Doc?" Oliver asked anxiously.

"Oh, that's right, I do owe you an apology," the doctor noted absently. "You see, my surgery was so deft and so skillful that when the operation was over all the gastroenterology students broke into spontaneous applause. And when I bowed, scalpel in hand, I happened to cut your dick off."

•

Herbie couldn't believe his luck when this beautiful medical student agreed to date him, and then to go to bed with him, and even to marry him. So when she graduated, they were married, and Herbie felt he was the luckiest man on earth—until he got suspicious that she was cheating on him.

So one day he decided to come home early from the night shift at the bottling plant. And when he entered his bedroom, Herbie found his naked wife in bed with the hospital's chief cardiologist. "Just what the hell do you two think you're doing?" he yelled.

"See," said his wife to the other doctor, "I told you he was dumb."

•

The aspiring psychiatrists were attending a lecture by an eminent specialist on manic depressives and their attendant emotional excesses. "As you know," began the professor, "the manic depressive careens from one extreme to the other. For instance, Mr. Hoskins, can you identify the opposite of agitation?"

"Serenity?" suggested the student.

"Very good. And of depression, Miss Ryan?"

"Elation."

"Indeed. And what, Mr. Taylor, is the opposite of woe?"

Mr. Taylor scratched his head. "Giddyap?"

•

Mickey wasn't worried by the chiropractor's reputation for roughness—but by the time he left, he'd signed one check and two confessions.

•

Casey made an appointment with a sex therapist and explained that he and his wife were unable to achieve simultaneous climax. "It's not a terrible problem, Doctor," he conceded, "but isn't there something I could do about it?"

The therapist confided that he and his wife had had the same problem, which he'd solved by hiding a pistol under his pillow. "When I was about to come, I reached for the gun and fired a shot, and Doreen climaxed with me. Come back next week and tell me how it works for you."

That very night the therapist got a call from the county hospital and rushed over to the emergency room. "What happened, Casey?" he cried, catching sight of his patient writhing in pain on an examining table, clutching a bloodsoaked towel to his groin.

Wincing, Casey explained that he'd gone right out to purchase a .45, hid it under the pillow, and started making love to his wife. "And when I was about to come, I grabbed the gun and fired."

"So?" pursued the doctor.

"She shat in my face and bit off the end of my dick."

•

The little old lady seated herself right behind the bus driver. Every ten minutes or so, she'd pipe up, "Have we reached Oriskany Falls, yet, sonny?"

"No, lady, not yet. I'll let you know," he replied, time after time. The hours passed, the old woman kept asking for Oriskany Falls, and finally the little town came into view. Sighing with relief, the driver slammed on the brakes, pulled over, and called out, "This is where you get out, lady."

"Is this Oriskany Falls?"

"YES!" he bellowed. "Get out!"

"Oh, I'm going all the way to Albany, sonny," she explained sweetly. "It's just that my daughter told me that when we got this far, I should take my blood pressure pill."

*　•

The hulking lumberjack came into the surgeon's office and said firmly, "Dr. Dunne, I want you to castrate me."

"Castrate you? That's a pretty odd request from a big, masculine fellow like yourself," the doctor pointed out. "Have you really thought this through, maybe talked to a therapist?"

"No questions," ordered the lumberjack. "I got no time to waste in chitchat. Here's your money— now get on with the operation!"

So the doctor had him strip, cleaned his groin with antiseptic, administered a general anesthetic, and duly castrated the patient. As the fellow was coming to, Dr. Dunne leaned over and suggested, "Since you're already here on the operating table, would you like me to circumcise you, too?"

"Goddamn it, Doc," cried the lumberjack, now a contralto, *"that's* the one I wanted done, *that's* the word!"

•

"I'm terribly worried about my son," confessed Mrs. Applegate to a psychiatrist friend of the family. "I came home early one day and caught him in the rec room with little four-year-old Emily from next door . . . and they both had their pants down."

"This sort of curiosity is very natural, Mrs. Applegate," the psychiatrist reassured her. "Try not to worry."

"I just can't help it," she sniffed. "And my son's wife's all upset, too!"

•

It took three years for Shelley to wise up to the fact that going to a psychiatrist wasn't doing her any good at all: now she was broke, when to start with she'd only been cracked.

•

What's the difference between a genealogist and a gynecologist?

A genealogist looks up your tree, while a gynecologist just glances into your bush.

•

The dentist was called away from the dinner table to take an urgent phone call. It was Mr. Tuckerman, explaining that young Junior had gotten himself into quite a fix. "See, he was kissing his girlfriend Corinne, and when my wife and I came back from the movies we found them stuck together."

"I'll come right over," said the dentist calmly, "and don't worry about a thing. I have to unlock teenagers' braces all the time."

"Yes, but from an I.U.D. and a ribbed condom?"

•

"Excuse me, sir," said the pharmacist politely to a big fellow buying a lottery ticket, "but I'm afraid cigar smoking isn't permitted on the premises."

The guy snorted, and exhaled a giant cloud of smoke. "I can smoke it if I want to, pal—after all, I bought it here."

"Big deal," returned the pharmacist coolly. "We sell Preparation-H too."

•

Did you hear what happened to the woman who swallowed a razor blade on Monday?

By Thursday she'd given herself a hysterectomy, castrated her husband, circumcised her boyfriend, and given her minister a harelip.

"For God's sake, *do* something, Dr. Weiss," screamed the desperate woman, shredding her handkerchief and pulling out hanks of hair. "Yesterday I thought I was a wigwam, today I'm convinced I'm a teepee . . ."

"Calm down, Estelle, calm down," soothed the psychiatrist. "You're just two tents."

•

Did you hear about the sex maniac who had asthma?

He could only catch his breath in snatches.

•

Handsome Vinnie had a great vacation visiting the back room of every gay bar on Castro and Christopher Streets, but it left him somewhat the worse for wear. When he got home he called up a friend who practiced homeopathic medicine and complained that his rectum was terribly swollen and tender. The friend recommended making a poultice of herbal tea leaves and applying it to the area, and it did relieve the irritation a bit.

But the next morning found Vinnie still in considerable discomfort, so he hobbled over to the office of a proctologist who served the gay community. In the examining room, the good-looking fellow bent over and spread his cheeks. The doctor clucked sympathetically and started investigating.

"Well, Doctor?" asked Vinnie after a few minutes had passed. "What's the diagnosis?"

"It's not completely clear, cutie," admitted the proctologist, "but the tea leaves *definitely* recommend a Caribbean cruise for the two of us."

.

"I'm glad you had the sense to follow my instructions exactly," remarked the pharmacist smugly. "Your cough seems much improved."

"It should be," replied the patient tartly. "I've been practicing it all night."

.

When Brewer woke up with his ankle all swollen and throbbing, he called Dr. Shrewsbury. "Soak it in hot water for an hour twice a day," was the physician's advice.

Brewer was watching a football game on TV and soaking his foot in a bucket of hot water when his wife got home from work, and when he explained what was going on, she snorted disbelievingly.

"That doctor's an idiot. An ice pack is what your ankle needs." So Brewer applied ice morning and evening, and in a few days he was as good as new.

That Saturday he ran into Shrewsbury at the hardware store and he couldn't resist telling him that his wife's advice had done the trick.

"Fine," responded Dr. Shrewsbury, clearly miffed, "but *my* wife says hot water."

•

During brunch at the yacht club, R. Chip Frothingham III took the family doctor aside and confided that he and his wife were having difficulty conceiving.

"I'm not a fertility expert, Chip, but maybe I can help," Dr. Gorham offered kindly. "What position are you in when you ejaculate?"

"Uh . . . what do you mean by ejaculation, Doctor?"

"When you climax?"

The young man still looked blank, so the doctor tried again. "When you come, Chip. Don't you come?"

Chip's face suddenly brightened. "Oh, do you mean that sticky white stuff, Dr. Gorham? Buffy thinks it's yucky, so I make sure to shoot it into the sink before getting into bed."

•

Why did the dentist spend his entire vacation in a whorehouse?

He wanted bigger cavities to drill.

•

Or the Marine dentist?

He always wanted to be on the drill team.

•

When Mrs. Owens made an appointment for her annual gynecological exam, she was informed that her old doctor had retired and the practice had been taken over by his associate, Dr. Krieg. Eager to hold on to such patients, young Krieg greeted her cordially. "Just pop those feet into the stirrups and scooch down a bit. This'll just take a jiffy," she rattled on cheerfully. "My, what a large vagina you have! What a large vagina you have!"

Mrs. Owens' composure was frayed. "You don't have to say it twice!" she snapped.

"I didn't say it twice. I didn't say it twice."

•

A fire swept through the building and Mr. Kornbluth was forced to jump from the roof in order to avoid being burned alive. Fortunately he landed in a privet hedge, but when he came to in the intensive care unit, the doctor was standing by the bedside with a worried look on his face.

"What's the story, Doc?" Kornbluth asked anxiously.

"You're going to live, I promise," the physician replied gravely, "but I must come right out and tell you that we had to amputate both legs above the knee."

"Oh, no." The poor patient turned his face to the wall until he'd regained his composure.

"But there's a bright side, Mr. Kornbluth," the doctor continued when he turned back. "You had *terrible* corns, and they'll never bother you again."

•

Why did the gynecologist quit medicine to become a stand-up comedian?

He decided it was time to see men crack up too.

•

Patient: "Doctor, nobody ever listens to me."
Shrink: "Who's next?"

111

Patient: "Doctor, I think you should know there's an invisible man in your waiting room."
Shrink: "Tell him I can't see him now. Next."

•

Patient: "Doctor, I'm feeling a bit schizophrenic."
Doctor: "That makes four of us. Next."

•

The man came into the psychiatrist's office, reclined on the couch, and told the doctor he needed help ridding his mind of an obsession. "All I can think of, day and night, is making love to a horse. It's driving me nuts."

"I see," said the shrink, rubbing his goatee. "Now would that be to a stallion or to a mare?"

"A mare, of course," retorted the patient, indignantly pulling himself upright. "What do you think I am, a pervert or something?"

•

"Dr. Bernard completely cured my hemorrhoids," Betty informed the other girls in the secretarial pool. "How'd he do it? First he had me bend over, of course, and then he put one hand on my shoulder and stuck the other up my. . . . Hang on a sec." Betty's face screwed up in concentration, and then she went on. "Yeah, that's it: Dr. Bernard put his right hand on my shoulder and stuck his left up. . . ."

Betty paled, and she gasped, "Wait just a minute! He had *both* hands on my shoulders."

•

As a routine part of his examination, the psychiatrist administered a Rorschach test to her newest patient. To his growing dismay, she noted that the young man associated every single picture with some sort of extreme sexual perversion. "I'm scheduling you in on Tuesday and Thursday afternoons at three o'clock," concluded the doctor firmly. "You need expert professional assistance on a long-term basis."

"Sure, Doctor, anything you say," agreed the guy cheerfully, "as long as I can borrow those dirty pictures over the weekend for the Girl Scout Jamboree."

•

"You're in excellent health, Mrs. DiMaggio," pronounced the doctor with a smile at the conclusion of her annual physical. "Is there anything else I could help you with?"

Mrs. DiMaggio nodded, then blushed. "You know how Sam is about doctors, he'd never ask you about this, Dr. Olofson . . . but he's been having trouble with impotence. Is there any medication that could help him?"

"Of course," said the doctor, and wrote out a prescription which Mrs. DiMaggio filled on the way home. Unfortunately the pharmacist made a mistake typing the label, putting "3 Tb" instead of "3 tsp," and when Dr. Olofson got into the office the next morning his phone was ringing off the hook. It was a frantic Mrs. DiMaggio.

"What's wrong?" asked the doctor. "Didn't the prescription work?"

"I'll say!" she cried. "Now I need an antidote so they can close the lid on the coffin!"

•

Did you hear about the lion who consulted an eminent Beverly Hills psychiatrist?

The king of the beasts complained that every time he roared, he had to sit through a two-hour movie.

•

The newlyweds went to spend Thanksgiving with her parents in Connecticut, and on the way back home they ran out of gas in a godforsaken part of the Bronx. When the fellow decided to head out in search of a gas station or pay phone, his bride sobbed, "Honey, don't leave me here. I'll get mugged—I'll get raped!"

"Nah," he said, opening the door. "Tell 'em the car broke down on the way to the V.D. clinic."

•

Who says there's no such thing as an honest doctor? What about the one whose nurse asked, "What are we operating for, Dr. Anderson?"

"Five hundred dollars," he replied.

"What I mean, Doctor, is what does the patient have?"

"Like I said, five hundred dollars."

•

"Ladies and gentlemen," queried the medical-school teacher, "today I would like you to consider what could be done for a child born without a penis. Yes, Mr. Dennis?"

"I'd wait till she was sixteen and give her one," responded the student brightly.

"Great news, Mr. Oscarson," the psychiatrist reported. "After eighteen months of therapy, I can pronounce you finally and completely cured of your kleptomania. You'll never be trapped by such desires again."

"Gee, that's great, Doc," said the patient with a sigh of relief.

"And just to prove it, I want you to stop off at Sears on the way home and walk the length of the store. You'll see—you'll feel no temptation to shoplift whatsoever."

"Oh Doctor, how can I ever thank you?"

"Well," suggested the doctor, "if you do have a relapse, I could use a microwave."

•

The Helmsleys were shown into the dentist's office, where Mr. Helmsley made it clear he was in a big hurry. "No fancy stuff, Doctor," he ordered. "No gas or needles or any of that stuff. Just pull the tooth and get it over with."

"I wish more of my patients were as stoic as you," said the dentist admiringly. "Now, which tooth is it?"

Helmsley turned to his wife. "Open wide, honey."

The woman came in to the podiatrist's office with the complaint that her feet always hurt. He asked her to walk down the hall and back so he could observe her, and when she sat back down in his office he pointed out that she was extremely bow-legged. "Have you been that way for a long time?" the podiatrist inquired.

"Nah," she answered, "not until recently. I've been screwing a lot doggie fashion."

"Well, I think you're going to have to switch to another position."

"No way," snapped the patient. "That's the only way my Saint Bernard will fuck."

•

"Tell me the truth, Dr. Hill," said the emaciated fellow. "How much longer am I going to live?"

"It's always hard to predict," she replied brightly, "but let's just say that if I were you, I wouldn't start watching any miniseries on TV."

Would you like to see your favorite tasteless jokes in print? If so, send them to:

Blanche Knott
c/o St. Martin's Press
175 Fifth Avenue
New York, NY 10010

We're sorry to say that no compensation or credit can be given. But I *love* hearing from my tasteless readers.

B. K.

The series that redefines the meaning of the word "*gross*"!

Blanche Knott's
Truly Tasteless Jokes

Over 4 million copies of *Truly Tasteless Jokes* in print!

TRULY TASTELESS JOKES IV
_____ 90365-0 $2.95 U.S.   _____ 90366-9 $3.50 Can.

TRULY TASTELESS JOKES V
_____ 90371-5 $2.95 U.S.   _____ 90372-3 $3.50 Can.

TRULY TASTELESS JOKES VI
_____ 92130-6 $3.50 U.S.   _____ 92131-4 $4.50 Can.

TRULY TASTELESS JOKES VII
_____ 90765-6 $2.95 U.S.   _____ 90766-4 $3.95 Can.

TRULY TASTELESS JOKES VIII
_____ 91058-4 $2.95 U.S.   _____ 91059-2 $3.95 Can.

TRULY TASTELESS JOKES IX
_____ 91588-8 $3.50 U.S.   _____ 91589-6 $4.50 Can.

Publishers Book and Audio Mailing Service
P.O. Box 120159, Staten Island, NY 10312-0004

Please send me the book(s) I have checked above. I am enclosing
$ _____ (please add $1.25 for the first book, and $.25 for each
additional book to cover postage and handling. Send check or money
order only—no CODs.)

Name _____
Address _____
City _____State/Zip _____
Please allow six weeks for delivery. Prices subject to change without
notice.   TTJ 8/89

READ

MY

LIPS.

The Wit & Wisdom of

GEORGE
BUSH

With some reflections by Dan Quayle

edited by Ken Brady & Jeremy Solomon

THE WIT & WISDOM OF GEORGE BUSH
Brady & Solomon, eds.
_____ 91687-6 $2.95 U.S.   _____ 91688-4 $3.95 Can.

Publishers Book and Audio Mailing Service
P.O. Box 120159, Staten Island, NY 10312-0004

Please send me the book(s) I have checked above. I am enclosing
$_____ (please add $1.25 for the first book, and $.25 for
each additional book to cover postage and handling. Send check
or money order only—no CODs.)

Name_____

Address _____

City _____ State/Zip _____

Please allow six weeks for delivery. Prices subject to change
without notice.

BUSH 9/89